The
Roaring
Twenties

Other books in the History Firsthand series:

The Civil War: The North
The Civil War: The South
The Constitutional Convention
The Gold Rush
The Great Depression
The Holocaust: Death Camps
The Vietnam War
War-Torn Bosnia

HISTORY
FIRSTHAND

The Roaring Twenties

Stuart A. Kallen, *Book Editor*

Daniel Leone, *President*
Bonnie Szumski, *Publisher*
Scott Barbour, *Managing Editor*
David M. Haugen, *Series Editor*

Greenhaven Press, Inc., San Diego, California

Library of Congress Cataloging-in-Publication Data

The Roaring Twenties / Stuart A. Kallen, book editor.
    p. cm.—(History firsthand)
  Includes bibliographical references and index.
  ISBN 0-7377-0884-0 (pbk. : alk. paper)—
  ISBN 0-7377-0885-9 (lib. : alk. paper)
   1. United States—History—1919–1933. 2. United States—
  Social conditions—1918–1932. 3. United States—Social life
  and customs—1918–1945. 4. Nineteen twenties. I. Kallen,
  Stuart A., 1955– II. Series.

E784 .R63 2002
973.91—dc21   2001033209

Cover photo: © Hulton-Deutsch Collection/Corbis
Library of Congress: 85, 104, 137, 186, 201
National Air and Space Museum, Smithsonian Institution: 173

Copyright © 2002 by Greenhaven Press, Inc.
10911 Technology Place, San Diego, CA 92127

Printed in the USA

Contents

pay did not compensate for the grueling work and the unforgiving bosses.

and despised Prohibition, influential leaders such as Henry Ford publicly praised the alcohol ban and argued against its repeal.

Chapter 4: Roaring Good Times

Chapter 5: Fads and Fancy

Foreword

In his preface to a book on the events leading to the Civil War, Stephen B. Oates, the historian and biographer of Abraham Lincoln, John Brown, and other noteworthy American historical figures, explained the difficulty of writing history in the traditional third-person voice of the biographer and historian. "The trouble, I realized, was the detached third-person voice," wrote Oates. "It seemed to wring all the life out of my characters and the antebellum era." Indeed, how can a historian, even one as prominent as Oates, compete with the eloquent voices of Daniel Webster, Abraham Lincoln, Harriet Beecher Stowe, Frederick Douglass, and Robert E. Lee?

Oates's comment notwithstanding, every student of history, professional and amateur alike, can name a score of excellent accounts written in the traditional third-person voice of the historian that bring to life an event or an era and the people who lived through it. In *Battle Cry of Freedom*, James M. McPherson vividly re-creates the American Civil War. Barbara Tuchman's *The Guns of August* captures in sharp detail the tensions in Europe that led to the outbreak of World War I. Taylor Branch's *Parting the Waters* provides a detailed and dramatic account of the American Civil Rights Movement. The study of history would be impossible without such guiding texts.

Nonetheless, Oates's comment makes a compelling point. Often the most convincing tellers of history are those who lived through the event, the eyewitnesses who recorded their firsthand experiences in autobiographies, speeches, memoirs, journals, and letters. The Greenhaven Press History Firsthand series presents history through the words of first-person narrators. Each text in this series captures a significant historical era or event—the American Civil War, the

Great Depression, the Holocaust, the Roaring 20s, the 1960s, the Vietnam War. Readers will investigate these historical eras and events by examining primary-source documents, authored by chroniclers both famous and little known. The texts in the History Firsthand series comprise the celebrated and familiar words of the presidents, generals, and famous men and women of letters who recorded their impressions for posterity, as well as the statements of the ordinary people who struggled to understand the storm of events around them—the foot soldiers who fought the great battles and their loved ones back home, the men and women who waited on the breadlines, the college students who marched in protest.

The texts in this series are particularly suited to students beginning serious historical study. By examining these firsthand documents, novice historians can begin to form their own insights and conclusions about the historical era or event under investigation. To aid the student in that process, the texts in the History Firsthand series include introductions that provide an overview of the era or event, timelines, and annotated bibliographies that point the serious student toward key historical works for further study.

The study of history commences with an examination of words—the testimony of witnesses who lived through an era or event and left for future generations the task of making sense of their accounts. The Greenhaven Press History Firsthand series invites the beginner historian to commence the process of historical investigation by focusing on the words of those individuals who made history by living through it and recording their experiences firsthand.

Introduction

U nlike most other decades in American history, the 1920s has many colorful nicknames. People call the years between 1920 and 1930 the Roaring Twenties, the Flapper Era, the Jazz Age, the Lawless Decade, and even the Era of Wonderful Nonsense.

Its many descriptive names well earned, the Roaring Twenties were unique in American history. It was the only decade completely under Prohibition, when the sale and manufacture of beer, wine, whiskey, and every other alcoholic beverage were illegal. Prohibition did not prevent tens of millions of Americans from imbibing anyway, but it did make them criminals in the eyes of the law. This widespread lawlessness was coupled with a booming economy that elevated the standard of living of the average middle-class American to new heights. And the lives of most people were profoundly changed by relatively new inventions such as inexpensive automobiles, the radio, and electrical appliances such as toasters, washing machines, vacuum cleaners, and other consumer goods.

The Bloody Prelude

The social and economic structure of the Roaring Twenties was forged in 1917, when the United States was drawn into World War I in Europe. Four million American men were drafted and 2 million U.S. soldiers went to fight in the bloody trenches of France, Belgium, and Germany in what was called "the war to end all wars." When World War I ended on November 11, 1918, over 10 million people had been killed, including more than a quarter-million Americans. Immediately after the war an influenza epidemic swept the globe and killed more than twice that number. As the new decade dawned, Americans were left shocked by the unprecedented destruction of the war and the indiscriminate death caused by the pandemic. As historian Bruce Catton writes in *American Heritage:*

> The . . . war, which had been so much more cataclysmic than any-body had imagined any war could be, was over, but it left smol-dering wreckage all over the landscape. . . . The certainties the adult American was used to . . . —the basic assumptions about world society which he had always taken for granted—were ob-viously either gone forever or rapidly going. Europe, which had always seemed to be the very center of stability, had collapsed. . . . Europe was [now] a center of disorder. . . .

> There was an immense, all-pervading disillusionment. The na-tion's highest ideals had been appealed to during the war, so that to win the war seemed the holiest of causes; the war had been won, but it was hard to see anything worth winning had been gained; the idealism had been used up, and the people had an un-easy feeling that they had been had.[1]

The Era of Silent Cal

During the war President Woodrow Wilson had promised to "make the world safe for democracy."[2] After the war, how-ever, Americans lost what little interest they had in policing the world, and instead elected Republican Warren G. Hard-ing, a small-town newspaper publisher from Ohio, who promised to return the country to what he called "normalcy."

Although Harding was known as an easygoing and ami-able leader, his administration was rife with corruption. Several of his advisers committed suicide when they were caught stealing public funds. And his secretary of the in-terior, Albert Fall, arranged for the private development of a federally owned oil field called Teapot Dome in Wyoming in exchange for a one-hundred-thousand-dollar bribe. The resulting scandal, known as the Teapot Dome affair, weakened Harding's administration and also his health.

Harding died suddenly of a heart attack on August 2, 1923, and was succeeded by Vice President Calvin Coolidge, known as "Silent Cal" for his extremely low-key demeanor—in fact, Coolidge was known to spend up to four hours each working day napping. Silent Cal's approach to government could be summed up in his famous expression, "The business of America is business,"[3] and the president's hands-off approach to federal regulation was a factor in the booming twenties economy.

The Power Age

In the aftermath of the world war, with Europe in collapse, America was the most powerful country on earth. And many whose religious convictions had been severely tested by the war's destruction turned to a new faith—materialism, business, and mass consumption. Business boosters attributed American prosperity and know-how to a higher power, and many believed it was true.

Another type of power also appeared on a grand scale in the 1920s. Gone were the days of gas lighting, hand-cranked record players, and iceboxes kept cool with huge chunks of ice carried to the door by icemen. The United States turned on the lights in the twenties as the proportion of homes supplied with electricity jumped from 20 percent in 1919 to 63 percent in 1927. This amazing new source of power allowed consumers to plug in radios, refrigerators, toasters, sewing machines, washing machines, and other electrical appliances.

Factories, too, utilized electricity to increase productivity and improve methods of manufacturing. As Harold U. Faulkner writes in *From Versailles to the New Deal:* "Electricity was the most powerful and efficient servant which mankind had yet subjected to his needs, and the factory power plant or public utility central station became the life center of many communities."[4]

The Tin Lizzy

While electricity made life easier, nothing changed the American landscape more than the famous Model T Ford automobile, or "Tin Lizzy," which cost only about $440 by the middle of the decade.

The first primitive automobile was invented in the late 1890s, and the Model T had been in production since 1908, although only 18,600 of the cars were sold that year. Even by 1915, there were less than 2.5 million cars in a nation of 100 million people. By 1920, however, over 9 million Americans owned cars; by 1930, that number had skyrocketed to 26.5 million. In addition to Fords, Americans bought Chevrolets, Cadillacs, Oldsmobiles, Packards, Duesenbergs, Pierce-Arrows, and cars with such now-obscure names as Excelsior, Kissel, Locomobile, and Roamer.

In *The Century,* Peter Jennings and Todd Brewster assess the impact of these cars:

> The burgeoning automobile age established a new sense of freedom and individuality: people no longer had to make their plans according to train schedules, and they traveled not with hundreds of strangers, but by themselves or with family and friends. At the same time, it also established a new, wider sense of community: small towns and villages that existed miles away from anyplace else were now connected to each other by roads, granting people who had long lived in isolation the opportunity to enjoy up-to-date medical care, higher-quality education, and whatever else lay "down the road."

> Thanks to the car, thousands of new suburban communities flourished, providing people with the luxury of homes surrounded by green grass even if they now had to commute to their jobs in the big cities. And the car allowed Americans to make their first major forays into tourism, forcing a country of "regions" to meld together and break down differences that once sharply divided not just North from South or East from West but one town from the next as well.[5]

With the advent of widespread automobile travel, the American landscape quickly changed. Before the war most roads in America were little more than dirt paths that turned into deep, sticky mud in the rain. With millions of people buying cars, citizens demanded that politicians build roads—and fast. By the end of the decade, federal, state, and city governments spent more money on highway building than on any other budget item except education.

Laced with winding concrete ribbons of highway the American countryside was quickly transformed from its centuries-old rural character. Pastures, forests, and fields were suddenly dotted with tourist cabins, gas stations, roadside diners, hot dog stands, and used-car lots.

The first grouping of stores known as a shopping center was built in Kansas City, Missouri, in 1924. The first "motor hotel," or motel appeared in San Luis Obispo, California, in 1925. The first parking garage was constructed in Detroit in 1929.

With the good came the bad as traffic jams, air pollution, and automobile accidents became commonplace. To improve safety, the first traffic lights were installed in New York City in 1922.

Prohibition

More and more Americans were driving, and some of them caused deadly accidents while drunk. For this and many other publicized reasons, the U.S. Congress, under pressure from an influential temperance movement and other conservative interests, passed the Eighteenth Amendment to the Constitution in 1919, which states: "No person . . . shall manufacture, sell, barter, transport, import, export, deliver, furnish, or possess any intoxicating liquor."[6]

The amendment, known as Prohibition, or the Volstead Act after the Minnesota senator who sponsored it, was doomed from the start. Almost as soon as the law went into effect on January 16, 1920, thousands of people set out to thwart it.

America's wide-open borders were a liquor smuggler's paradise. As Jules Abels explains in *In the Time of Silent Cal:*

> There were 18,700 miles of land and sea to patrol, a hopeless task. Ships loaded with liquor left Vancouver in Canada charted for Mexico and returned empty in twenty-four hours, obviously having got rid of their cargo near Seattle or Portland. Detroit faced Canada across the mile-wide Detroit River, and wholesale smuggling by speedboat made it the liquor capital of the world. . . . [Foreign] ships [loaded with liquor] stood in a line 12 miles off our

shore, called Rum Row, where they were met at night by [smugglers'] speedboats, often 75 feet in length and capable of going 50 miles an hour, enabling them to outrun any Coast Guard boat.[7]

As the price of an illegal drink shot up from twenty-five cents to two dollars or more, tens of thousands of illegal bars, called speakeasies, opened in nearly every village, town, and city. In some neighborhoods of Chicago, there were dozens of speakeasies on every block.

Those who couldn't afford brand-name "booze" could manufacture their own. Grocery stores sold beer ingredients such as malt, hops, and yeast in a bucket from which an amateur home brewer could make his or her own beer. Others simply added yeast to grapes or other fruit to make their own wine. Those who wanted a more potent beverage could make "bathtub gin" by pouring grain alcohol—used for industrial purpose—into a bucket with various herbs and flavoring.

To counter this widespread opposition to the law, the government appropriated $2 million to fight bootleggers, speakeasy owners, and smugglers. This sum was dwarfed,

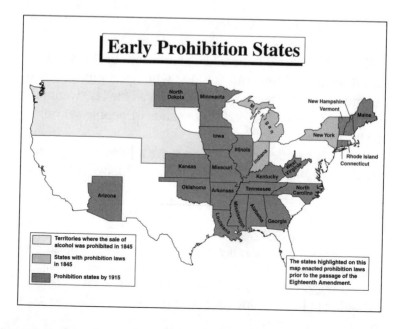

Early Prohibition States

Territories where the sale of alcohol was prohibited in 1845

States with prohibition laws in 1845

Prohibition states by 1915

The states highlighted on this map enacted prohibition laws prior to the passage of the Eighteenth Amendment.

however, by the $2 billion Americans were willing to spend every year to get drunk. And no single person sopped up more of this illegal money than the biggest bootlegger in the United States—Al "Scarface" Capone.

The Chicago-based Capone controlled an army of 700 thugs to oversee his empire of 11,000 speakeasies, hundreds of "rum running" boats, and dozens of warehouse breweries. To maintain his power, the gangster ordered approximately 400 murders of rivals every year. He doled out millions of dollars to police officers, judges, and politicians who allowed him to operate unhindered in Chicago and vast areas of the Midwest. Few of the 3,000 federal Prohibition agents, who earned a paltry $3,000 a year, could resist the bribes offered to them by the likes of Capone and his organized crime colleagues.

Morals and Flappers

With criminals such as Capone supplying illegal booze, the simple act of drinking a martini became an exciting adventure for millions of Americans. And the covert thrill of drinking helped fuel a widespread youth rebellion that spread throughout society.

In earlier decades young men were expected to be conservative, industrious, and hard working. Young ladies were expected to be prim, proper, modest, and virtuous. The war, however, had changed all that.

Many young men who had served in Europe had been exposed to the sophisticated ways of Europeans who openly drank and smoked in outdoor cafés. In addition, Europeans had a relaxed attitude toward sex that was new to American youth.

Women's fashions were also influenced by Europeans, as small, helmetlike cloche hats, short dresses, made-up faces, silk stockings, short "bobbed" hair, and long strings of beads became all the rage. And every fashionable woman wore a pair of unbuckled galoshes that "flapped" when she walked, inspiring people to call her a flapper.

Although these simple changes of fashion seem harmless, the flappers stunned the more conservative members of the populace. Author Clancy Strock comments on this phenomenon in *From Flappers to Flivers:*

> It's hard for us today to appreciate how deeply traditionalists were shocked when women decided to "bob" their hair. Outraged fathers stalked out of the house. Grandparents were scandalized. Husbands were speechless. Ministers thundered that it foretold a total breakdown in national morality.
>
> Worse still, women began showing their legs as hemlines soared up, up, up . . . nearly to the knee. Before the Twenties, a brief flash of ankle as a lady alit from a carriage was about as much excitement as onlooking men could handle. But now . . . !
>
> Women showed up on tennis courts unencumbered by long dresses. Bathing suits were actually brief enough for swimming. What was the world coming to?[8]

Flapper fashions were only part of the shocking 1920s youth rebellion. The Roaring Twenties ushered in an era of women's liberation as teenage girls across America took up drinking, smoking, and driving automobiles in unprecedented numbers. In fact, cigarette sales doubled during the twenties mainly as a result of women picking up the habit.

Sunday church was replaced by movies or long rides in convertibles, many of which had "rumble" seats in the trunk area. Cars full of flask-swilling teenagers sped down country roads, women shrieking with delight, men playing silly songs on ukuleles, while farmers and pedestrians wondered what was happening to America's youth.

The First Sexual Revolution

Sex, in any age, can always be counted on to titillate the public. In the 1920s, however, it seemed sex was everywhere. Theatrical plays and vaudeville skits often were based on sexual themes, and theaters were sometimes shut down by vice squads for showing "obscene" entertainment. Books, too, were becoming more risqué, and it was up to the post office—which kept a list of over five hundred banned titles—to stop this perceived obscenity from being sent through the mail.

Some moralists blamed the sexual revolution of the twenties on the father of modern psychiatry, Sigmund Freud. Although the Austrian psychiatrist completed his most important work, *The Interpretation of Dreams,* in 1900, his theories became part of popular culture in the United States after World War I.

Freud believed that sexual repression was the cause of most neurosis, and this belief was quickly adopted, and adapted, by middle-class Americans. According to the wry observations of Frederick Lewis Allen in *Only Yesterday: An Informal History of the Nineteen-Twenties:*

> [The] more-or-less educated public was now absorbing quantities of popularized information . . . which gave a general impression that men and women were merely animals of a rather intricate variety, and that moral codes had no universal validity and were often based on curious superstitions. A fertile ground was ready for the seeds of Freudianism, and presently one began to hear even from the lips of flappers that "science taught" new and disturbing things about sex. Sex, it appeared, was the central and pervasive force which moved mankind. Almost every human motive was attributable to it: if you were patriotic or liked the violin, you were in the grip of sex—in a sublimated form. The first requirement of mental health was to have an uninhibited sex life. If you would be well and happy, you must obey your libido. Such was the Freudian gospel as it imbedded itself in the American mind after being filtered through the successive minds of interpreters and popularizers and guileless readers and people who had heard guileless readers talk about it. New words and phrases began to be bandied about the cocktail-tray . . . inferiority complex, sadism, masochism, Oedipus complex. Intellectual ladies went to Europe to be analyzed; analysts plied their new trade in American cities, conscientiously transferring the affections of their patients to themselves; and clergymen who preached about the virtue of self-control were reminded by outspoken critics that self-control was out-of-date and really dangerous.[9]

The obsession with sex led to an obsession with appearance, especially among women, who flocked to neighborhood beauty parlors for the first time. Such establishments had been available to wealthy women for years, but the number of beauty shops that catered to average women quadrupled during the Roaring Twenties. For the first time, working women could get permanents, manicures, and pedicures at a reasonable price. The thin look was in, and unlike earlier decades when fat was thought to indicate wealth, American women went on diets using the newly invented bathroom scale to keep track of their weight.

Under the Influence of Movies

Little did more to influence American fad and fashion than the glamorous people portrayed in the silent films of the 1920s. In earlier decades, movies were short and plots were simple. The twenties represented a golden age in Hollywood, however, and films became two- to three-hour epics featuring wildly popular stars such as Charlie Chaplin, Douglas Fairbanks, Clara Bow, and Lillian Gish.

Latin lover Rudolf Valentino, whom writer H.L. Mencken called "catnip to women"[10] was the biggest sex symbol of the decade and was credited for the fact that 60 percent of movie audiences were female. The influence of Valentino and other movie stars on the general public was profound. As Jennings and Brewster write:

> [People] look to the movies for guidance on how to dress, talk, smoke, and appear sexy. Girls mimicked vamps like Theda Bara and copied the sexual gestures of Clara Bow (the "It" girl). Joan Crawford encouraged the craze for flappers. After Valentino became a big hit with his performance in *The Sheik,* college-aged men wore baggy-style Valentino pants, called themselves "sheiks" and the women, "shebas."[11]

When Valentino died from a massive stomach infection in 1926 at the age of thirty-one, over one hundred thousand people, many of them weeping women, mobbed his funeral in New York City.

Movie Palaces

Fans of Valentino and other twenties movie stars flocked to theaters that had grown nearly as glamorous as the movies themselves. By mid-decade more than twenty thousand theaters were scattered across the country, most built to feature live stage shows and project first-run films for only fifty cents per ticket.

Movie theaters were big, ornate, and garish, built to resemble the Taj Mahal, royal French palaces, ancient Greek gardens, or Chinese pagodas. The grandest theaters featured huge pipe organs, and even thirty-piece live orchestras, to provide dramatic music during the silent films. Ushers wore uniforms with gold braids and epaulets that rivaled those of decorated generals. After the first "talkie" film, *The Jazz Singer,* was introduced in 1927, theaters sprouted booming sound systems.

John Margolies and Emily Gwathmey describe the work of one popular theater architect in *Ticket to Paradise: American Movie Theaters and the Fun We Had:*

> The pioneer of the ingenious "atmospheric" auditorium was John Eberson. Beginning . . . in 1923, the Austrian-born architect created indoor "stars and clouds" stage sets simulating open-air amphitheaters. Side walls were replete with windows; facades and rooftops were adorned with a plaster menagerie of gods, goddesses, hanging vines, stuffed birds, and mysterious statuary. Above it all twinkled a glorious moonlit sky and lazily drifting clouds, formed by a smooth plaster ceiling . . . painted deep blue and pricked with hundreds of pinholes. The illusions of nature in an Italian garden, a Persian court, a Spanish patio, or mystic Egyptian temple yard was intensified by an imaginative lighting system capable of coloring in sunrise to sunset.[12]

Flagpoles and Fads

Going to the movies and imitating the appearance of movies stars was just one trend in a decade when people went crazy for fads. With the economy humming along at a brisk pace, Americans seemed almost desperate to entertain themselves in novel ways. In 1924 a movie stuntman named Alvin "Shipwreck" Kelly climbed atop a flagpole for more than thirteen hours in Los Angeles, and started a nationwide fad. In the months that followed Kelly's stunt, one man sat high atop a flagpole in Denver for twelve days. Another broke that record and lasted twenty-one days on a flagpole in Los Angeles. Kelly finally set the world record in 1929 by staying aloft for forty-nine days on a flagpole in Atlantic City, New Jersey, where over twenty thousand people came to watch some portion of the event.

Those who bored easily watching a man sit on top of a flagpole could find entertainment in watching people dance for days—or even months on end, at dance marathons.

Beginning in 1923 dance marathons were major attractions in dozens of cities across America. Dancing couples with large numbers on their backs competed for prizes of one thousand to five thousand dollars. This sadistic contest is described by Andrew Marum and Frank Parise in *Follies and Foibles: A View of 20th Century Fads:*

> Serious marathoners danced for months at a time in a crowded hall or in a crowded section of a fairgrounds. They were allowed only a 15-minute rest period after every hour (in the last stages of the marathon, this was sometimes shortened to 3 minutes); were poked at by the judges, who watched everything going on on the floor closely to make sure the contestants didn't fall asleep: and were taunted by the master of ceremonies to go faster. Yet the marathoners kept it up—for a number of reasons. There were those who saw the contest as a way to earn money; this was true of many marathoners during the midst of the Depression, which started in 1929. There were also marathoners who were trying to make it as entertainers and saw the grind as an opening to establish some contacts by showing how good they were. There were people running away from dullish former lives and people who thought they would be able to find a marriage partner in the dance marathons, (this did happen, always accompanied by great publicity from the marathon promoters and the newspapers). And there were people who did it for the fun of it—to prove to themselves how long they could take it.[13]

When people weren't watching dance marathons and flagpole sitters, they were entertaining themselves with other 1920s fads such as crossword puzzles, Ouija boards, and a Chinese game of skill known as mahjong. These games became popular nearly overnight, were embraced by millions, and faded from prominence nearly as fast as yesterday's news.

The Music of Black America

Whether at dance marathons or speakeasies, jazz music filled the air. It floated out from radios in bars and beauty parlors and it was played by live bands at dance halls.

The word *jazz,* a black slang term for making love, was on everybody's lips. Fashionable clothes were called "jazz dresses," modern syncopated verse was called "jazz poetry," and fast old cars were called "jazzy jalopies."

Jazz was real American music, combining elements of ragtime, marching band music, and blues. Born in the black neighborhoods of New Orleans around 1895, jazz traveled with African American musicians up the Mississippi River to Kansas City and Memphis, and over to Chicago, eventually hitting it big in New York City in the twenties.

Like so much else during the decade, the spread of jazz throughout popular culture can be attributed to Prohibition. Before alcohol was outlawed, there were few saloons in America where black and white people mixed. But the gangsters who ran speakeasies hired black jazz musicians to attract adventurous young white people, who spent freely and danced to suggestive new dances named the Black Bottom and the Charleston.

Jazz was improvised music—the musicians invented melodies around a basic framework of notes. This defiance of traditional musical rules fit well with the spirit of the twenties generation. The music, like the era, was erratic, eccentric, fast, feverish, and exciting. Band leader Paul Whiteman, who called himself the "King of Jazz," called it "the folk music of the machine age,"[14] but perhaps virtuoso pianist Fats Waller defined it best when he stated: "Man, if you don't know what it is, don't mess with it."[15]

In spite of Waller's humorous warning, twenties music lovers—both black and white—could not stay away from jazz music. Musicians such as Louis Armstrong, Cab Calloway, Duke Ellington, Bessie Smith, King Oliver, and others played to packed houses and sold millions of records while inspiring a new generation of musicians to improvise original tunes. As critic J.A. Rogers wrote in *Survey* magazine in 1925:

> Jazz has come to stay because it is an expression of the times, of the breathless, energetic, superactive times in which we are living. . . . The Negro musicians of America are playing a great part in this change. They have an open mind, and unbiassed outlook. They are not hampered by conventions or traditions, and with their new ideas, their constant experiment, they are causing new blood to flow in the veins of music. The jazz players make their instruments do entirely new things, things finished musicians are taught to avoid. They are pathfinders into new realms.[16]

Most white patrons of black jazz clubs did not think of the music in such a highbrow way, however. These people simply wanted to put the stuffy "Victorian" age behind them and enjoy the sounds of what black bandleader Duke Ellington called the "jungle sound."

And the music was not without its harsh critics. The mixture of sensuous dancing, bootleg liquor, and the mixing of races prompted antijazz crusader Ann Shaw Faulkner to say, "Jazz was originally the accompaniment of the voodoo dance, stimulating half-crazed barbarians to the vilest of deeds."[17]

The Harlem Renaissance

Racist critics such as Faulkner were threatened not only by jazz music, but by the growing creative output among black poets, painters, authors, historians, playwrights, and traditional musicians. And just as Harlem was an important center of the jazz movement, it was also the birthplace of what was called the "New Negro" movement, or the Harlem Renaissance. Urged on by black leaders such as Marcus Garvey and W.E.B. Du Bois, African Americans, who faced grinding poverty and discrimination, were encouraged to celebrate their talents and their racial heritage.

The movement's most outspoken leader was West Indian–born Marcus Garvey, who, as a dark-skinned black, considered light-skinned African Americans to be inferior. To support this position, Garvey refused to carry advertisements for skin lighteners and hair straighteners in his newspaper, the *Negro World.* Garvey's other controversial positions included support of segregation and opposition to interracial marriage. He preached that Christ was black and that all of the world's civilizations originated in black Africa. Garvey even started a program to return American blacks to Africa.

Garvey's Universal Negro Improvement Association (UNIA) attracted thousands of followers, who also took part in the New Negro movement by buying books by writers such as Langston Hughes and Dorothy West, and by supporting the work of painters such as Jacob Lawrence, Henry O. Tanner, and William Henry Johnson.

Roaring Backlash

Not every American was enthralled with the Harlem Renaissance, bootleg liquor, flappers, and "jivin'" jazz music. In fact, blatant overt racism was rampant in the United States, spurring, especially in rural areas, a bloody backlash to the "New Negro" and other modern concepts.

Throughout the twenties, nearly half of the people in the country lived in rural areas and these citizens, disdainfully referred to as "boobs and yokels"[18] by popular writers such as Sinclair Lewis, remained firmly in control of American politics. Prohibition was an excellent example: Of the 197 congressmen who voted for the Volstead Act, 129 were from small towns of less than ten thousand people. As Sinclair Lewis wrote, "National prohibition was a measure passed by village America against urban America."[19]

The most obvious demonstration of rural racism and political power was in the explosive growth of the Ku Klux Klan throughout the decade. In 1920, Edward Young Clarke and Elizabeth Tyler, a couple of clever business boosters, revived the nearly extinct Ku Klux Klan and turned it into a multimillion-dollar business. They signed up members from ads in men's magazines, and sold Klan memberships for ten dollars apiece.

In a multilevel marketing scheme, local operators, called Kealgles, made a few dollars each time they signed up members of a lower order called Goblins. The Goblins profited by signing up even more members from places such as local fraternal organizations like the Masons, Elks, and others.

While signing up only white, Protestant men, the Klan put forth programs that appealed to the prejudices of their members. According to Wyn Craig Wade in *The Fiery Cross: The Ku Klux Klan in America:*

> Kealgles were told to sell the Klan in a way that most appealed to the community. If the town was afraid of labor unions, then Kealgles pushed the Klan's opposition against alien-inspired strikers. If the Kealgle was working [where illegal alcohol was plentiful], he promised that the Klan and the Klan alone had the guts to deal with . . . bootleggers. If the city was being swollen by immigrants, Kealgles proclaimed that the Klan stood for 100 percent Americanism and would never allow the country be taken over by a pack of radical hyphens [such as Italian-Americans or German-Americans]. And when neighborhoods expressed fear over the postwar "New Negro," they were quietly reminded that the Ku Klux Klan had always known how to handle [blacks]. In short, Kealgles pandered to every regional prejudice and fear, offering a scapegoat for every local tension. Never before had a single society gathered up so many hatreds or given vent to an inwardness so thoroughgoing.[20]

By 1924 the Klan had over 4 million members, with the strongest chapters, called Klaverns, in Texas, Louisiana, Oklahoma, Arkansas, and Indiana. While Clarke and Tyler made hundreds of thousands of dollars the Klan set out on a rampage of terrorism against Asians in California, Mexicans in Texas, Jews in New York, and African Americans wherever they lived. On election days Klan members prevented black people from voting. Black men were lynched for supposedly looking at white women. White people who were friendly to blacks faced floggings.

In 1921, the New York *World* newspaper launched an investigation of the Klan and detailed 152 separate acts of murder, assault, and terrorism including, according to Wade, "four murders, forty-one floggings and twenty seven tar-and-featherings."[21]

Meanwhile the Klan installed governors and congressmen in at least six states. Politicians in some areas controlled by the Klan were forced to join a local Klavern. Future Supreme Court Justice Hugo Black was a Klan member, and Warren G. Harding became a member of the Klan in a private ceremony in the White House. Eventually money and power corrupted the Klan and by 1925 several top Klan leaders had been indicted on charges ranging from sexual assault to murder. As more people became educated to the real purpose of the Klan, its membership numbers dropped drastically.

Lindbergh Flies to Paris

By 1927 the rise and fall of the Klan, murderous Prohibition gangsters, and crazy fads such as flagpole sitting caused many Americans to wonder about the future of their country. To some it seemed as if the age of honor had ended in the bloody trenches of World War I. Americans needed a new hero, and they found one in Charles Augustus Lindbergh, the plain-speaking senator's son from Minnesota.

On the morning of May 20, 1927, Lindbergh climbed into his single-engine airplane, *Spirit of St. Louis,* and took off from Roosevelt Field on Long Island, New York. With only five sandwiches and a canteen full of water—and unable see over the 425-gallon gas tank in front of the cockpit—Lindbergh aimed his plane toward Paris. For the next thirty-three and one-half hours the pilot fought off sleep and heavy rain. At one point the turbulence was so bad that Lindbergh was forced to fly only ten feet above the ocean surface. After flying over Newfoundland and Ireland, and circling the Eiffel Tower in Paris, Lindbergh landed at Le Bourget airfield. He was shocked to discover that people on the ground had reported his progress and notified radio stations along the way. When he climbed out of the *Spirit of St. Louis,* nearly one hundred thousand joyous French people were cheering wildly.

As the first person to successfully make a solo transatlantic flight, Lindbergh became an overnight hero. When he returned to America aboard a navy carrier personally sent by the president to retrieve him, a ticker-tape parade in New York City broke attendance records. Over five thousand poems were published honoring Lindbergh and 250 songs were written about his flight. In the month after his return, the twenty-seven-year-old pilot received 3.5 million pieces of fan mail, many from young women proposing marriage. He was offered millions of dollars from advertisers and movie companies, but the clean-cut pilot refused all offers, preferring instead to tour the country giving patriotic speeches.

The Crash

The exuberance America felt while celebrating Lindbergh's accomplishment was probably the highest moment of the 1920s. But the party did not come crashing to a halt until Black Thursday—October 24, 1929, when the stock market began its long slide into the Great Depression. By Tuesday, October 29, American investors had seen over $14 billion evaporate—comparable to half the total amount spent fighting World War I.

The Great Crash took almost everyone by surprise. Throughout the twenties all major business indicators had been positive. Industrial production increased dramatically as consumers snapped up goods such as radios, refrigerators, and cars. Corporate profits had skyrocketed as new mass production techniques allowed companies to churn out goods cheaply and efficiently. And driven by the policies of Henry Ford, who believed that a well-paid employee could better afford a new Model T, workers were receiving better pay and working fewer hours.

Flush with cash, middle-class Americans went on a spree, believing that anybody could be rich with just a little bit of luck. Stories circulated in the press of shoeshine boys and nurses who invested in the market and made tens of thousands of dollars virtually overnight. Newspapers and magazines also reported on the land boom, in which speculators bought swampland for $20 an acre and sold it two months later for $2,000, or even $10,000. It seemed that the sky was the limit and the good times would never end.

Many who invested in the stock market bought shares on "margin," that is, stock paid for by money borrowed from the broker against the value of the stock. Some margin rates were as low as 10 percent, which allowed someone with $1000 to buy $10,000 worth of stock. When the stock value rose, the broker was paid off from the profits. But when stocks lost more than half their value at the end of October 1929, no one could pay their margin calls. When the money could not be repaid, brokers and banks were forced to shut their doors. People who had borrowed against their property lost their homes.

Although no more than 1.5 million Americans actually owned stocks, in a nation of about 120 million, the publicity surrounding the crash sent the country into a tailspin. Within weeks, factories shut their doors and unemployment began to climb. Millions of poor Americans—farmers, miners, textile workers, and others—were thrown out of work. As the 1930s dawned, the United States entered the Great Depression. Over 25 percent of American workers would lose their jobs in the coming decade, and the misery would not end until it was replaced by another calamity, World War II, in the early 1940s.

The Past and the Present

Although today the 1920s seem consigned to the distant past—a black-and-white time before televisions, cell phones, and computers—the fashions, foibles, and problems of that decade can still be seen in modern times. Then, as now, adults complained about the loose morals of the younger generation and their love of silly fads, crazy music, cigarettes, and illegal substances. The stock market soared to unprecedented heights and skidded to precipitous lows, wiping out the fortunes of average Americans who bought stocks that were ridiculously overvalued. Like the illegal drug trade today, Prohibition allowed violent gangsters to make millions of dollars by supplying a dangerous drug— in this case, alcohol—to insatiable consumers who refused to remain sober. And, unfortunately, racial prejudice and fear of foreigners were problems then and remain so today.

By looking past flapper fashions, rickety Model T Fords, and families huddled around the radio, it is possible to see the common humanity that binds the past to the present. People of the 1920s, like many today, believed that they lived in a modern age full of technological wonders. Most were optimistic and held a bright vision of the future, knowing that they lived in a rich nation where almost anything was possible. That belief echoes through the decades, through war, depression, peace, and prosperity from today's great-grandparents to young children who are just beginning to learn about American history.

Notes

1. Bruce Catton, "The Restless Decade," *American Heritage,* August 1965, p. 6.

2. Quoted in Milton Melzer, *Brother Can You Spare a Dime?* New York: Random House, 1969, p. 6.

3. Quoted in Melzer, *Brother Can You Spare a Dime?,* p. 6.

4. Harold U. Faulkner, *From Versailles to the New Deal.* Toronto: Glasgow, Brook, 1950, p. 108.

5. Peter Jennings and Todd Brewster, *The Century.* New York: Doubleday, 1998, p. 103.

6. Quoted in John Kobler, *Ardent Spirits: The Rise and Fall of Prohibition.* New York: G.P. Putnam's Sons, 1973, p. 215.

7. Jules Abels, *In the Time of Silent Cal.* New York: G.P. Putnam's Sons, 1969, p. 91.

8. Quoted in Bettina Miller, ed., *From Flappers to Flivers.* Glendale, WI: Reminisce Books, 1995, p. 10.

9. Frederick Lewis Allen, *Only Yesterday: An Informal History of the Nineteen-Twenties.* New York: Harper & Brothers, 1957, pp. 98–99.

10. Quoted in Jennings and Brewster, *The Century,* p. 127.

11. Jennings and Brewster, *The Century,* p. 127.

12. John Margolies and Emily Gwathmey, *Ticket to Paradise: American Movie Theaters and the Fun We Had.* Boston: Little, Brown, 1991, p. 22.

13. Andrew Marum and Frank Parise, *Follies and Foibles: A View of 20th Century Fads.* New York: Facts On File, 1984, p. 45.

14. Quoted in Ethan Mordden, *That Jazz! An Idiosyncratic Social History of the American Twenties.* New York: G.P. Putnam's Sons, 1978, p. 153.

15. Quoted in Mordden, *That Jazz!*, p. 153.

16. Quoted in George E. Mowry, *The Twenties: Fords, Flappers, and Fanatics.* Englewood Cliffs, NJ: Prentice-Hall, 1963, p. 66.

17. Cultural Shock: Music and Dancing, "Early Jazz 1900–1930," www.pbs.org/wgbh/cultureshock/flashpoints/music/jazz_at.html, 2000.

18. Quoted in Loren Baritz, *The Culture of the Twenties.* Indianapolis: Bobbs-Merrill, 1970, p. xxii.

19. Quoted in Baritz, *The Culture of the Twenties,* p. xxvi.

20. Wyn Craig Wade, *The Fiery Cross: The Ku Klux Klan in America.* London: Simon and Schuster, 1987, pp. 155–56.

21. Wade, *The Fiery Cross,* p. 160.

Chapter 1

An Economic Boom

Chapter Preface

After experiencing a deep recession at the end of World War I, the U.S. economy entered a period of extraordinary growth that was the hallmark of the Roaring Twenties. Between 1921 and 1929 the production of automobiles, radios, refrigerators, washing machines, vacuum cleaners, sewing machines, and other electrical appliances provided tens of thousands of jobs and sent the stock market soaring. Between 1923 and 1929 alone, the production of appliances tripled, while the numbers of electric refrigerators owned by consumers jumped from 27,000 to 755,000. Not only did these new inventions herald the beginning of the modern age, but they fueled an economy that allowed millions of Americans to live more prosperous lives than at any previous time in history.

Flush with cash, an unprecedented number of people turned to the stock market to make their fortunes. Speculation was fueled by newspaper and magazine articles, some that claimed it was every American's God-given right to get rich overnight without hard work. Often left unmentioned was the fact that the market was controlled by a few wealthy industrialists. Like a gambling casino, the house—in this case the bank or brokerage—always won, whether stock prices rose or fell.

Meanwhile, an unparalleled land boom in Florida was reflecting the roller-coaster ride of the stock market. Cheap swampland that had been considered worthless only a few years earlier was bought and sold like the hottest stocks. Investment money poured into Florida from across the country as people turned $2000 investments into $20,000 virtually overnight.

America's premier comedy team, the Marx Brothers, even made a slapstick movie about the madness called *Cocoa-*

nuts, in which Groucho Marx plays a Florida hotel owner desperately trying to unload real estate on unsuspecting buyers. In reality Groucho himself lost hundreds of thousands of dollars in the land boom when a 1926 hurricane blew away a million dreams of unlimited wealth.

Until the market crash of 1929, however, the harsh realities of the marketplace remained hidden from most people's view. The twenties economy roared onward, spiraling skyward, with no end in sight.

Business:
The New Religion

Edward Earle Purinton

In the 1920s, the business of buying, selling, working, and manufacturing was practiced with near religious fervor. In the following article, Edward Earle Purinton, business publicist and author of self-help articles, expounds on the popular twenties belief that business is the finest art, education, philosophy, and even religion.

Among the nations of the earth today America stands for one idea: *Business*. . . . For in this fact lies, potentially, the salvation of the world.

Through business, properly conceived, managed and conducted, the human race is finally to be redeemed. How and why a man works foretells what he will do, think, have, give and be. And real salvation is in doing, thinking, having, giving and being—not in sermonizing and theorizing.

I shall base the facts of this article on the personal tours and minute examinations I have recently made of twelve of the world's largest business plants: U.S. Steel Corporation, International Harvester Company, Swift & Company, E.I. du Pont de Nemours & Company, National City Bank, National Cash Register Company, Western Electric Company, Sears, Roebuck & Company, H.J. Heinz Company, Peabody Coal Company, Statler Hotels, Wanamaker Stores.

These organizations are typical, foremost representatives of the commercial group of interests loosely termed "Big

From "Big Ideas from Big Business," by Edward Earle Purinton, *Independent,* April 16, 1921.

Business." A close view of these corporations would reveal to any trained, unprejudiced observer a new conception of modern business activities. Let me draw a few general conclusions regarding the best type of business house and business man.

The Best Pursuit

What is the finest game? Business. The soundest science? Business. The truest art? Business. The fullest education? Business. The fairest opportunity? Business. The cleanest philanthropy? Business. The sanest religion? Business.

You may not agree. That is because you judge business by the crude, mean, stupid, false imitation of business that happens to be located near you.

The finest game is business. The rewards are for everybody, and all can win. There are no favorites—Providence always crowns the career of the man who is worthy. And in this game there is no "luck"—you have the fun of taking chances but the sobriety of guaranteeing certainties. The speed and size of your winnings are for you alone to determine; you needn't wait for the other fellow in the game—it is always your move. And your slogan is not "Down the Other Fellow!" but rather "Beat Your Own Record!" or "Do It Better Today!" or "Make Every Job a Masterpiece!" The great sportsmen of the world are the great business men.

The soundest science is business. All investigation is reduced to action, and by action proved or disproved. The idealistic motive animates the materialistic method. Hearts as well as minds are open to the truth. Capital is furnished for the researches of "pure science"; yet pure science is not regarded pure until practical. Competent scientists are suitably rewarded—as they are not in the scientific schools.

The truest art is business. The art is so fine, so exquisite, that you do not think of it as art. Language, color, form, line, music, drama, discovery, adventure—all the components of art must be used in business to make it of superior character.

The fullest education is business. A proper blend of study, work and life is essential to advancement. The whole man is educated. Human nature itself is the open book that all business men study; and the mastery of a page of this educates you more than the memorizing of a dusty tome from a library shelf. In the school of business, moreover, you teach yourself and learn most from your own mistakes. What you learn here you live out, the only real test.

The fairest opportunity is business. You can find more, better, quicker chances to get ahead in a large business house than anywhere else on earth. The biographies of champion business men show how they climbed, and how you can climb. Recognition of better work, of keener and quicker thought, of deeper and finer feeling, is gladly offered by the men higher up, with early promotion the rule for the man who justifies it. There is, and can be, no such thing as buried talent in a modern business organization.

The cleanest philanthropy is business. By "clean" philanthropy I mean that devoid of graft, inefficiency and professionalism, also of condolence, hysterics and paternalism. . . . Not so in the welfare departments of leading corporations. Savings and loan funds; pension and insurance provisions; health precautions, instructions and safeguards; medical attention and hospital care; libraries, lectures and classes; musical, athletic and social features of all kinds; recreational facilities and financial opportunities—these types of "charitable institutions" for employees add to the worker's self-respect, self-knowledge and self-improvement, by making him an active partner in the welfare program, a producer of benefits for his employer and associates quite as much as a recipient of bounty from the company. I wish every "charity" organization would send its officials to school to the heads of the welfare departments of the big corporations; the charity would mostly be transformed into capability, and the minimum of irreducible charity left would not be called by that name.

The Sanest Religion

The sanest religion is business. Any relationship that forces a man to follow the Golden Rule rightfully belongs amid the ceremonials of the church. A great business enterprise includes and presupposes this relationship. I have seen more Christianity to the square inch as a regular part of the office equipment of famous corporation presidents than may ordinarily be found on Sunday in a verbalized but not vitalized church congregation. A man is not wholly religious until he is better on week-days than he is on Sunday. The only ripened fruits of creeds are deeds. You can fool your preacher with a sickly sprout or a wormy semblance of character, but you can't fool your employer. I would make every business house a consultation bureau for the guidance of the church whose members were employees of the house.

I am aware that some of the preceding statements will be challenged by many readers. I should not myself have made them, or believed them, twenty years ago, when I was a pitiful specimen of a callow youth and cocksure professional man combined. A thorough knowledge of business has implanted a deep respect for business and real business men.

The future work of the business man is to teach the teacher, preach to the preacher, admonish the parent, advise the doctor, justify the lawyer, superintend the statesman, fructify the farmer, stabilize the banker, harness the dreamer, and reform the reformer. Do all these needy persons wish to have these many kind things done to them by the business man? Alas, no. They rather look down upon him, or askance at him, regarding him as a mental and social inferior— unless he has money or fame enough to tilt their glance upward. . . .

The biggest thing about a big success is the price. It takes a big man to pay the price. You can measure in advance the size of your success by how much you are willing to pay for it. I do not refer to money. I refer to the time, thought, energy, economy, purpose, devotion, study, sacrifice, patience, care, that a man must give to his life work before he can make it amount to anything.

The business world is full of born crusaders. Many of the leaders would be called martyrs if they weren't rich. The founders of the vast corporations have been, so far as I know them, fired with zeal that is supposed to belong only to missionaries.

Of all the uncompromising, untiring, unsparing idealists in the world today, none surpass the founders and heads of the business institutions that have made character the cornerstone. The costliest thing on earth is idealism.

Gambling on Wall Street

Fred C. Kelly

In the 1920s, millions of average Americans hoped to get rich buying and selling stocks on Wall Street. But some people, such as author and columnist Fred C. Kelly, saw that rich and powerful bankers stacked the odds against middle-class investors. For typical working-class citizens, investing in the market was little different than gambling in a casino where the house always wins. Unfortunately, Kelly's sage observations could do little to counter popular get-rich mob psychology that outweighed common business sense.

W all Street is a symbol for activities of powerful banking interests and of speculation in stocks and bonds. Yet the New York Stock Exchange is not even on Wall Street, but around the corner on Broad Street. Great banks are here, however, J.P. Morgan & Company, the National City Bank, the Bankers' Trust Company—powerful financial groups that are perhaps the real masters of the people. Headquarters of these vast banking interests are usually either on or *near* Wall Street. Hence when anybody undertakes to make money by speculating in securities—no matter how far he lives from New York—he is said to have put money into Wall Street. When he loses, as he probably does, it is said that the Wall Street boys took his money from him. Of course this form of gambling may be done anywhere, as New York brokers have branch offices all over New York,

From "Gambling on Wall Street," by Fred C. Kelly, in *America as Americans See It,* edited by Fred J. Ringel (New York: Harcourt, Brace, 1932). Reprinted by permission of the author.

all over the United States, and even aboard great ocean liners where reports are sent by radio for the benefit of those who have gone traveling in quest of change and surcease [pause] from business cares.

Most of the largest brokerage houses which buy and sell securities for customers on commission have their main offices, however, either on Wall Street or within gunshot of it. Tradition is that they must usually be at least on the east side of Broadway and south rather than north of Wall Street. Because of the great rental pressure for space in skyscrapers in this locality, it is said that within recent years the increased value of land in the Wall Street region exceeds the value of all the gold taken out of California since the great gold rush of 1849.

Legal Gambling

Since many forms of gambling, including horse-racing, are prohibited in various parts of the United States, the Wall Street game has become almost the universal and favorite national excitement by all classes of people, from humble clerk to multimillionaire. As Dr. John B. Watson, eminent psychologist, says: "Even sex has become so free and abundant in recent years that it no longer provides the thrill that it once did, and gambling in Wall Street is about the only real excitement that we have left."

So great is this national vice of trying to beat Wall Street that before the great stock panic of November 1929, it was estimated that more than a million dollars each day were paid to brokers in commissions alone for executing the orders of those who buy and sell stocks—a million a day to the kitty!

It is well known that, in the long run, the great majority of people who fool with Wall Street lose their money. During the last year, thousands of men and women who had been living on little legacies, or on life savings, found themselves penniless. They had gone into Wall Street in a small way and then kept throwing good money after bad, until finally all they had was gone. As nearly as can be ascertained, not more than two or three persons in each hundred who try to take money out of Wall Street, are successful. Thus we find that the percentage of successful speculators is just about the same as the percentage of genuinely intelligent people who show up in any so-called intelligence test—whether in the army, in college, or wherever such tests are made.

No Place for Normal Behavior

Let us now look to see just why so large a proportion of all who try their luck in Wall Street, should lose.

Most people who attempt to take profits from Wall Street, lose their money for the simple reason that they are normal people. Normal behavior is hopelessly unsuited to speculative success. Wall Street has its bait designed to catch the greatest number—and the greatest number are average folk. Hence the danger of behaving in the market as an average, normal person does.

I don't believe the prime requirement is intelligence so much as an ability to place one's self in a frame of mind where it is possible to distrust one's own natural impulses and go contrary to them. We must make up our minds to become cautious and fearful at the very time we are inclined to feel most hopeful—and to show courage when we are scared. We must go contrary to the common belief. The greatest cause of panics is the belief that there can't be one. It is this belief which makes it possible for big powerful interests to place over-priced stocks in weak hands. When the rank and file realize that they have bought stocks—partly on borrowed money—that are likely to sell at much lower prices, all wish to sell at once—and that, of course, is a panic.

One couldn't well do anything more normal than to buy stocks at top prices and sell out later at the exact bottom—for that is what the majority of speculators do, and it is altogether logical that they should, since it is when stocks are high-priced that we hear the most encouraging news about them. Indeed, that is why they advanced to the top figures—because of all this favorable news constantly drummed into people's ears. Reversing the process, the normal person is especially likely to sell at the exact bottom because it is then that the news is worst. What could be more logical than to become disgusted with a stock and sell it when you hear nothing but bad news about its present and future outlook?

We often think it is a strange coincidence that just after we sell *our* stock it quits going down. The price we take isn't the bottom just because *we* sold there—but because a great mass of other people sold there. The reason so many other people picked the same day and about the same price that we did is because they are just like us—average folk. Whatever news in the papers, or other propaganda, that influenced one person influenced all the others. Because human nature is much the same wherever found, it always responds to the same kinds of stimuli. The more normal we are, the more nearly average, the more likely we are to buy or sell when the biggest group of others do.

Now, it must be obvious that this great mass of speculators must in the long run always be wrong, or else there wouldn't *be* any such stock market as we now know. Let us suppose that right now many decided bargains are available. If they are really bargains and everybody were intelligent enough to recognize them as such, then everybody would try to buy them. This buying would have a tendency to force prices upward, and the bargains would not long exist. Likewise, when prices are too high, shrewd people sell. Hence, if everybody were truly clever, prices would never go as high as they do now; the minute they went beyond real values, everybody would start to sell. The consequence of all this would naturally be that prices, never going sensationally high or low, would stay within a narrow range—indeed, in such a narrow range that it might not pay speculators to monkey with the market at all. Possibly there would no longer be a stock market.

The Game Is Always Rigged

Every successful speculator knows, every broker knows, and every student of human psychology knows, that the mass of people are overwhelmingly less intelligent than the few. All scientific intelligence tests, in the army, in schools and colleges, everywhere, indicate that about two per cent of all the people in any community are more capable of reaching logical conclusions than are the other ninety-eight per cent. One may easily prove this simply by checking over his own list of acquaintances. You probably know at least one hundred persons fairly well. You may know several hundred; but of this list, you naturally know one hundred better than the others. Now, of this one hundred intimate friends, neighbors and other acquaintances, aren't there two or three who have far more sense, whose opinions on almost anything you would rather trust, than all the rest put together? No matter

Boom Market Humor

Will Rogers was a humorist and actor famous for his witty, down-to-earth commentaries on American life. He often wrote about the unfathomable antics of the stock market, which was building up to an incredible high before the great crash of 1929. When Republican president Calvin Coolidge was elected in 1924, stock values rose to unprecedented levels. In his inimitable style, Rogers questions why stocks would actually be worth so much more only twenty-four hours after the election.

We are able to report much jubilation on the part of the disgracefully rich, or Republican, element of the entire country. They are celebrating the country's return to Wall Street.

And stocks, why, anything that looked like a stock would sell. People would wire in, "Buy me some stocks." The broker would answer, "What kind?" The buyer would wire back, "Any kind; the Republicans are in, ain't they all supposed to go up?"

Men bought stocks who had never even bought a toothbrush before. People bought wheat and sent a truck to the [Stock] Exchange to get it. . . .

Personal fortunes have been made. I read of one who cleaned up 10 million in cast iron pipe. Here cast iron pipe has been laying around for years and we never thought much

how many people you start running around a race track, they can't overtake a champion, can they?

Surely it is reasonable to assume that the stock market has lured in a fairly representative cross-section of the public and that, therefore, if the majority of all people are less capable than the few of deciding anything sensibly, this must hold true likewise of their behavior in stocks. In fact, it is even more true of people in the market, because of highly and skillfully organized plans to lead them astray. The game is always rigged by the smart to outwit the stupid.

---

of it. It was all right to hit someone over the head with, or to stumble over, and here all it needed was a president from Vermont to put it on its feet. You know it is really remarkable how near cast iron pipe is linked up with New York's 45 electoral votes.

Coca-Cola took a jump right out of the glass. That seems kinder strange that a summer drink stock should wait until November to show its value. Thought we elected Mr. Coolidge to lower our taxes and keep us at peace with the world. I didn't know that we had to drink Coca-Cola.

International Harvester was another. Now harvesters are all in the sheds and will be until next June; still, people are just crazy about them, even idle. What makes these things worth so much more on November 5th [the day after the election] than they were on November the 3rd? I was old-fashioned enough to think that supply and demand regulated the price of everything. Now I find November the 4th regulates it. Who is going to pay all these extra profits these things are supposed to earn?

You mean to tell me that in a country that was really run on the level, 200 of their national commodities could jump their value millions of dollars in two days? Where is this sudden demand coming from all at once?

Will Rogers in *Will Rogers' World,* Bryan B. Sterling and Frances N. Sterling, eds. New York: M. Evans, 1989.

To succeed in the market, then, one must *not* do what most others are doing. Hence it is dangerous to pay the slightest heed to what one most often hears or sees . . . regardless. But since most people are fairly sure to be wrong, he who does the *opposite* has a good chance to be right. We may not *know* what the highly intelligent minority are doing, but by watching and studying the crowd, we can pick up useful clues as to what that same minority are *not* doing. In other words, those of us who are only moderately intelligent and might not behave wisely by independent effort, always have the opportunity to join up with smart folk if we'll just consistently pay no attention to all the signs which say: Follow the Crowd!

The only trouble with this formula of doing the opposite from the crowd is that one isn't always sure what the crowd really is doing and, anyhow, it is not so easy as it sounds to go in the other direction even if one does know. When all our neighbors, our favorite financial pages, and all other agencies, keep drumming it into us that one line of action is wisdom, such thoughts become so merged with our own, if we ever had any of our own, that the line of least resistance is to do what everybody says.

The idea of making money by coppering the bets of the crowd, is not, however, a mere theory, for it is exactly what Big Operators do. Men of wealth and power who have enough important contact with banks and other sources of information to know exactly what is going on, back-stage, are able to tell when any stock or any group of stocks are over-bought. When the public is too deeply in the market, on margin accounts, these Big Operators know that the market is top-heavy. They say the *technical position* is poor. It is just the time for them to sell . . . for they know that prices *must* go down.

Good Old Uncle Greed

A brief outline of the average man's behavior in a good advancing market where there is plenty of opportunity for profits, is something like this: Buys timidly at first, very little, if any, at low prices, but gains confidence as advance continues and buys more. He takes small profits, but noting that stocks still advance, he is sorry he sold and buys back same stocks higher up. This time he determines to get more profit, waits too long to sell and stock starts to decline. Then he mistakes each lower price for a bargain and buys more to even up. Later he gets scared and sells entire holdings for less than lowest price he paid. And remember that for each transaction he must contribute a fee to the kitty! Thus it is easy to lose a fortune even in an advancing market.

The Big Boys who successfully outwit the crowd in the market have learned much of human psychology. True, many of them might not know how to spell psychology; but they understand it. They know that a man's worst enemies in the market are: His vanity, his greed, his will to believe whatever he *hopes* is true, and his sheep instincts, that is, his desire to follow the crowd.

Perhaps the worst enemy of all is vanity. People lose because they hang on and refuse to admit that they were mistaken in buying what they did or when they did. They take small profits but large losses because of this unwillingness to sell at a *small* loss and frankly admit that they were wrong. (This unwillingness to admit when we're wrong is what causes half the troubles in the world. It causes lawsuits; it throws good people into divorce courts; it is the greatest cause of murder and wars.) It is vanity that makes people believe too much misinformation. They believe what isn't true rather than even consider the hypothesis that they might be fooled.

Next to vanity, I presume a person in the market should guard most cautiously against having his judgment warped by old Uncle Greed. If I had only sold every stock I ever bought at the price I expected to receive at the time I bought it, I should be far better off? Many a time I have placed a selling order on the same day I got the stock, but when the stock had about reached my price, canceled the order—because I decided that a few hundred dollars' profit wasn't nearly enough. And, without a single exception, every time I have thus canceled a selling order placed before my greed got to working on me, the stock later went down and I sold it below the figure I had at first planned to take.

Sad words are these:—oh, if I had only sold when—! But we all use them. Because we all have our human share of greed, it is always harder to make up one's mind to sell than to buy. Every broker knows that not one-tenth as many customers will take warning and get out of the market, when urged to by some one in whom they have faith, as would take the same man's advice on the buying side. The explanation is that you buy because you see a chance to make money, but when you sell out you abandon hope of further gain. Greed!

The Will to Believe

After vanity and greed, perhaps the most malign influence to one trying to make money from the market is the Will-to-Believe. We think to be true whatever we hope is true. When a reputable doctor tells a man he has an incurable disease, the man is then quite likely to fall into the hands of a quack who says *he* can cure him. He wouldn't believe the quack ordinarily, but now, if he doesn't believe, his only hope in life is gone. Likewise, men pin their faith to poor stocks and expect these to advance 40 or 50 points, because here is their last hope of financial salvation.

Perhaps more stock market phenomena are due to psychological than to economic causes. You may have noted that the high price of a stock for a certain period is more frequently 99 or 145, than 100 or 150. This is, presumably, because human beings have learned to think in round numbers. Nearly everybody says: "I'm going to keep my stock until I get 100 for it," and that very thing may prevent the stock from reaching that point. Too many want the big round price, and stick to it. Hence most of the demand near that figure is satisfied by those willing to take just a wee bit less—99 or even 99⅞. Nearly always when a stock sells at 100 for the first time, it immediately goes a little higher, because considerable pressure was required to push it to 100 and this same pressure is likely to carry it still farther.

A definite psychological explanation exists for the fact that, all other items being equal, stocks are more likely to be weaker on Monday than on other days. Men worry about their stocks on Sunday and their wives, noting this worry, urge them to sell the next day. Then, too, if men go to church there is additional reason to be pessimistic, since preachers round-up sinners by fear far more frequently than by hope, and don't paint any too pretty a picture of the future.

It might not be so difficult to derive profit from the Wall Street game if it weren't for human nature. If one were to buy good stocks whenever the market ceases to go down on bad news and sell when it ceases to go up on good news, he should do well. But human psychology places obstacles in the way. Nearly everybody has his own brand of mental hazard which keeps him from stepping into the money. It may be that he is too impatient to buy or too reluctant to sell. Usually it's both of these. Most important of all, he must never lose sight of the fact, no matter what he hears or sees, that the *crowd is always wrong!*

Florida Land Boom and Bust

A.M. Sakolski

> While the stock market rose dramatically throughout the
> 1920s, thousands of average Americans became millionaires
> at a time when a new car Model T Ford cost only four hun-
> dred dollars. No one imagined that it would all come crashing
> down in 1929, except perhaps, A.M. Sakolski, assistant pro-
> fessor of finance at the College of the City of New York.
>   Sakolski observed the Florida land-boom hysteria between
> 1924 and 1926 firsthand, and wrote about what can happen
> when speculation, greed, and a frenzy for profits overtake
> reality in the marketplace. While thousands of "get-rich-quick"
> investors were wiped out by the Florida land boom and bust,
> it was only a small precursor to the crash that would follow.

How did it start? No one can give a completely satis-
factory answer. Yet its origin is not a mystery! For several decades Florida was the nation's winter playground.
From millionaires down to farmers, all classes of the population made vacation visits there. The wheat growers of the
West found it an opportune place to pass the idle and dreary months when their lands lay fallow. The capitalists of the
North found it a convenient country in which to escape the
rigors of severe winters, and to relax from business cares.
Florida beaches and Florida camps thus became notable
health resorts. The tropical vegetation, and the semitropical
climate were alluring. It was something different from the
environment of almost every other part of the nation.

Excerpted from *The Great American Land Bubble,* by A.M. Sakolski (New York: Harper
& Brothers, 1932).

What could be more natural, then, while passing hours of idleness in this national winter playground, than the purchase of a winter home or a large tract of land there? One becomes "an easy mark" during vacations, and is apt to spend more lavishly and purchase more liberally than when at home. Countless Florida tourists became Florida real estate proprietors. The millionaires bought large estates; the lesser rich bought town and beach lots.

Interest was thus accumulated in Florida real estate. Those who bought told others of their purchases. Millionaires would not be outdone by other millionaires. Rivalry and jealousy led to acquisitions of Florida "estates" and to the engrossment of large and favorably situated tracts. Moreover, the Florida waste and unoccupied lands could be bought relatively cheap, compared with land values in more settled industrial and farming sections. There were immense stretches of undeveloped coast lands and countless acres of untilled soil that were continually on the market. Much of this was held in large acreages by individual owners, and could be readily acquired at wholesale. Florida, in this respect, was "America's last frontier."

Because of these conditions, public attention was centered on Florida real estate. Just one large, well-advertised "promotion scheme" could set the pot of speculation boiling.

Vast Schemes of Development

Another factor leading to the recent outburst of speculation in Florida was the creation of transportation facilities there. The Florida East Coast Railroad, a monumental enterprise conceived as a millionaire's hobby, was completed in 1900. It opened up for settlement a vast area, relatively unoccupied, in the southern part of the peninsula. As its traffic grew, it enlarged its equipment. Other railroad lines were constructed on both east and west coasts. In addition, new and improved highways were cut through. The Everglades were in process of being drained by state and local appropriations. Steamship lines also aided. Thus, the frontier character of the territory was changed. As in the western country, a "boom" followed the creation of transportation and communication facilities.

The boom was not a sudden outburst. There were rumblings for several years. Vast schemes of development were set on foot. The draining of the Everglades, the building of a canal and harbor at Lake Worth, the development of Palm Beach, the planning of Coral Gables and a hundred other projects gave a favorable setting. The year 1924 marks the beginning of the rush period. It followed the first mass invasion of real estate promoters and "developers," though many had arrived by means of peaceful penetration for several years previous. The climax was reached in 1925. In 1926 came the collapse.

Who were the instigators of the fiasco, and who were responsible for its execution?

The original promoters were all men of mark. There was Henry B. Plant, who came to Florida as early as 1861, and who built railroads and hotels there. He founded Plant City, a successful real estate development. Next, there is Henry M. Flagler, Standard Oil executive, who visited Florida in 1885. The possibilities of the state as a winter playground were revealed to him. He built at St. Augustine, the Ponce de León and the Alcazar hotels, dreams of massive architecture. His creative ambitions broadened. He built the Florida East Coast Railroad—a marvelous, though foolhardy engineering feat—and adorned its lines with palatial hotels. He also bought heavily of Florida lands. "Flagler Street," the principal thoroughfare in Miami, and the headquarters of the late, though not lamented, real estate fraternity, is an adequate reminder of this master builder's benefactions to the Peninsula State. Then, there is Barron Collier, the advertising magnate, who developed a whole county that bears his name. This county was established in 1923 and embraces over 1,200,000 acres. When he acquired it, the land had never been touched by plowshare or other human tools.

Collier started to make his vast estate a garden spot, building roads, draining swamps and establishing a town. He invested his millions in these ventures and persuaded others to do the same by this proof of his faith in them. In speaking of the great future of Collier County, and its increasing population, he once remarked, poetically: "The light of the fireflies will be dimmed by the electric lights in happy homes, and the chirp of the katydids will be chorused by the laughter of happy children."

Many others contributed to Florida's expected greatness. The "Great Commoner" and perennial presidential candidate, William Jennings Bryan, made his residence there. Although his limited wealth prevented him from entering upon great development schemes, his contribution was equally effective, for his pen and his masterful voice gave extremely valuable aid and encouragement. Roger W. Babson, stock market forecaster and dispenser of voluminous statistics, also lent a hand. J.C. Penney, merchant and philanthropist, and John and Charles Ringling, circus operators, likewise contributed capital and enterprise, and raised their voices in praise of the Land of the Everglades. Others of this type, such as T. Coleman DuPont, August Heckscher and Jesse Livermore, could be mentioned, but it is not necessary to furnish a full list. When millionaires, statesmen and investment counselors—men of repute, foresight and discretion—added the weight of their influence to the persuasions of ordinary professional real estate promoters, then it was no wonder that the population went mad over the fabulous possibilities of pecuniary gain in the scrub lands and everglades of the Florida peninsula.

Suckers Are Born Every Minute

Thus encouraged by the aid of shrewd and enterprising capitalists, and by the nascent prosperity following in the wake of the post-war depression, the Florida people vigorously laid out the groundwork of the "boom." In March, 1925, there was convened at West Palm Beach a meeting of the representative business men from all parts of the state. Needless to say, the "real estaters" and "developers" were there in force. They organized themselves into the Florida Development Board and committed themselves to spend a

million and a half dollars or more, if necessary, for publicity during the next five years. They began a series of boosting advertisements, art pamphlets, books and all other de-
vices to attract the fortune seeker as well as the tourist to the
confines of the state. Tourists and fortune seekers are almost
indistinguishable. Tourists have surplus funds, otherwise
they could not travel, and a goodly proportion of those who
went to Florida merely for a holiday came back property
owners and local taxpayers. One could hardly venture outside his hotel room in a Florida resort without stumbling
over a half dozen high pressure real estate salesmen.

The advertising campaign of the Florida Development
Board, assisted by the Florida land and real estate mortgage
companies, brought to their aid the magazines and the press.
Articles describing the allurements of the "American Riviera," the "Nation's Winter Playground," "America's Winter
Paradise," as well as the immense agricultural, mineral and
industrial resources of Florida, appeared in the leading liter-
ary and business periodicals. They occupied prominent positions in the Sunday editions and "travel numbers" of the
newspapers. At the height of the excited boom, the *Saturday
Evening Post,* the most widely read of American popular periodicals, began a Florida series by Thomas McMorrow and
Kenneth Roberts, and continued them at almost regular in-
tervals throughout the period of the boom.

Even after the "crash" came, following the hurricane
which swept away the paper fortunes of multitudes, the
"boosting" continued. Florida would not only recover, but
a new and greater period of prosperity would be ushered in.
"The suckers will not stop coming," one could almost read
between the lines. "They have made only a beginning of
buying into Florida. Those who lost their 'binders' may be
discouraged, but there are others. Suckers are born every
minute, and some can still be induced to put their savings in
resurrected swamp lands and wind-swept beaches."

When the host of real estate promoters, gathered from all
parts of the United States, concentrated in Florida, then the
real boom was on. Most of these mongers were not "to the

manor born." They were like the "carpetbaggers" of the
South in post–Civil War days. They came to fill their pock-
ets, not to make the country rich. They cared not whom they
duped, nor what became of their projects when once they
had unloaded them. The foolish mortals who hung around
their "offices," and paid for "binders," "options" and "con-
tracts," were merely fish in their nets. Nor were they, in
many cases, merely "crooked dealers." As already noted, the
vast "developments" engineered during the boom period had
the backing of great names in present-day financial circles.
There were among these men many who transferred their
activities from stock market operations or legitimate real estate dealings in settled communities to a field where they
saw opportunities of greater profit. When the collapse came,
they withdrew and resumed their former occupations. . . .

Buying Swampland

Of course, every development in Florida was to be a "city,"
and the lots were sold before the project was even launched.
This is well described by Mr. Walter C. Hill, vice-president
of the Retail Credit Company of Atlanta:

> Lots were bought from blue prints. They look better that way.
> Then the buyer gets the promoter's vision, can see the splendid
> curving boulevards, the yacht basin, the parks lined with leaning
> coconut trees, and flaming hibiscus. The salesmen can show the
> expected lines of heavy travel and help select a double (two-lot)
> corner for business, or a quiet water-front retreat suitable for a
> winter home. To go see the lot—well,—it isn't done. Often it is
> not practicable, for most of the lots are sold "predevelopment."
> The boulevards are yet to be laid, the yacht basin must be pumped
> out, and the excavated dirt used to raise the proposed lots above
> water or bog level. Then they will be staked, the planning done,
> and the owner can find his lot.

Whenever a new "development" was conceived, the promoters immediately advertised it in the newspapers and by
handbills, giving descriptions of the location, extent, special
features and the approximate prices of the lots. Reservations

were made by depositing 10 per cent of the proposed price, and these reservations were taken up in the order received, and attended to before the regular sale of lots was opened. The holder of the reservation was thus permitted to select from a beautifully drawn plan, on which lots and prices were marked, the sites he desired. He then got a "binder," i.e., an option on the selected lot, which he could resell immediately. This gave him a thrill, for he felt that he was the owner of Florida real estate—even if actually in a swamp— and he hoped to transfer his "purchase" at a fabulous profit to an absentee or latecomer. . . .

An enumeration of all the "developments" in Florida during the years 1924–26 would cover many pages. These stretched for hundreds of miles both north and south of Miami. They covered the west coast of the state from the southerly tip up to and beyond Cedar Keys. And fancy names they had, too! The Spanish language appears to have been quite an advertising asset to the "developers." Pasadena, Santa Monica, Buena Vista, Rio Vista, and other pleasant sounding appellations, so agreeable to Californians, were adopted, as well as names from Italy, such as Naples, Venice, Indrio, Riviera, and those of other famous Mediterranean resorts. Common Spanish terms were even adopted, such as "Los Gatos" (the Cats) and "Boca Raton" (Rat's Jaw), hideous in the vernacular but, of course, high sounding, since the real meaning was unknown to most of the speculators.

Every important city, town or "development" had its slogan. Miami was "The Magic City"; Orlando, "The City Beautiful"; Hollywood, "The Golden Gate of the South"; St. Petersburg, "The Sunshine City"; and Fort Lauderdale, "The Tropical Wonderland." Indrio, a development that never "panned out," was called "Florida's Newest and Most Beautiful," although it is still largely a wind-swept stretch of sand and scrub. And Hollywood, "Golden Gate of the South," leads to nowhere. Coral Gables, the largest of the projected "cities," was to be the "Venice of America." To make the slogan effective, its promoters are said to have actually imported

Venice-built gondolas, and expert gondoliers were expressly ordered to complete the architectural *motif*. . . .

Boom Goes Bust

Undoubtedly, some instigators of the Florida boom, especially those who bought and resold early in the proceedings, realized handsome profits. Several "millionaire winter residents," who previously had bought estates merely for their personal enjoyment, later sold to "developers" with fabulous gains. On the other hand, others who contracted the speculation fever, and endeavored to undertake developments on their own account, lost heavily. But aside from individual gains and losses, the boom period was one of great prosperity in Florida. Its wealth, as measured in current values, increased in a short period of two years to tremendous proportions. From 1923 to 1926, the state's population . . . increased from 1,057,400 to 1,290,350, or 22 per cent, and bank deposits from $225,000,000 to $850,000,000. . . . The transportation facilities were inadequate to handle the passengers and goods which poured into the state in the excited days of rising real estate values. The effect was a high cost of living, high rates of wages and inadequate living quarters.

When these obstructions to material progress were being seriously encountered, the clouds of recession began to gather on the horizon. The frenzied activities of the summer and fall of 1925 were carried over into 1926, but the eagerness of speculators to bid up values began gradually to disappear. . . .

The same benign Nature which made Florida the "Land of Flowers" and "An Earthly Paradise," reversed the process [of development]. As in years past, on September 9, 1926, a terrific West Indian hurricane blew over the southern portion of the peninsula and interrupted the dreams of "easy money" which the very atmosphere seemed to have engendered during the preceding three years. The debacle was complete. The hordes of real estate developers, high pressure salesmen, feature writers and private "investors," which had invaded the territory "in Pullmans [train cars] and

Packards [automobiles]," were now confronted with desolation and despair. They hastily departed.

The banks were drawn on heavily, and their swollen deposits faded away. From a high level of $850,000,000 at the end of 1925, deposits in Florida banks dropped to $550,000,000 at the end of 1926, and reached still lower figures thereafter. An epidemic of bank failures was the result. Florida real estate mortgages, with "security a certainty," were a drug on the market. One "development" after another lapsed. Installment payments on lots practically ceased. The bubble had burst!

There were a few attempts at resurrection. The state authorities even decried the publication of the extent of the hurricane damage, because of its discouraging effects on land values. An effort was made to turn away the Red Cross from its relief work. Newspapers and magazines were told that Florida's marvelous progress would continue. A typical statement was contained in the *Wall Street Journal,* October 8, 1926. It quoted Mr. Peter O. Knight, of Tampa, counsel of the Seaboard Air Line Railway, as saying: "The same Florida is still there with its magnificent resources, its wonderful climate, and its geographical position. It is the Riviera of America, and always will be, within twenty-four hours or less, of eighty millions of prosperous people, and the same causes which developed Florida so rapidly in the last few years, will cause a greater and more permanent Florida to be developed in the future."

Chapter 2

An Unequal Society

Chapter Preface

Times were great for middle-class Americans in the 1920s, but a vast gulf existed between the rich and the poor. While industrialists such as Henry Ford and John D. Rockefeller earned tens of millions dollars annually, the average millworker or miner brought home only about forty dollars a month. And without union protection, many factory workers labored sixty hours a week under unbearably harsh sweatshop conditions.

Those who protested or tried to form unions to fight back were labeled communists by bosses and politicians who feared that an organized workforce might rise up and take over the factories. These worries were not entirely unfounded. In 1917 communist revolutionaries, known as Bolsheviks, toppled the Russian government, killed Czar Nicholas II and his family, and began an era of dictatorial rule. As the communists raised the red flag over the Russian capital in Moscow, a "Red Scare" spread to America.

This panic was fueled by large numbers of immigrants who had moved to the United States in waves between 1890 and 1920. Italians, Jews, Slovenians, and other Eastern Europeans flocked to big cities such as New York, Cleveland, Detroit, Chicago, changing the face of American culture. This frightened some Americans, especially in rural areas, where the Ku Klux Klan became a force to be reckoned with.

The Klan was founded in 1866 after the Civil War in order to terrorize and subjugate newly freed African Americans in the South. Under intense government pressure, the Klan all but disappeared in the late nineteenth century. The Klan was revived when it was romanticized in the 1915 film *The Birth of a Nation,* by director D.W. Griffith. By portraying Klan members as heroes, the film prompted a new Klan that gained popularity by preaching anti-Catholic, anti-Jewish,

antiblack, antisocialist, and anti–labor union "Americanism."
Under dynamic new leadership the Klan grew into a large
and powerful organization of 4 million members, including
congressmen, governors, and even the president of the United States.

During the same time, a renaissance of black pride and
culture was taking place in New York City's Harlem neighborhood. The harsh realities of being an African American
were the topics of many poems, books, new articles, and
countless discussions that came out of the Harlem Renaissance. The movement's political figurehead was a West Indian immigrant named Marcus Garvey, whose Back to
Africa Movement urged black Americans to even move back
to Africa and build a new settlement untainted by prejudice.
Although racial tensions had always run high in the United
States, during the Roaring Twenties, prejudice was exacer-
bated by the Red Scare and the preaching of segregationists
both black and white.

Living on Thirteen Dollars a Week

Paul Blanshard

> While many Americans lived comfortable lives in the 1920s
> economic boom, farmers and factory workers saw their
> incomes decline as the cost of living soared. In the following
> excerpt, an unnamed cotton mill worker in Greenville, South
> Carolina, describes her life to reporter Paul Blanshard. The
> article appeared in *The Nation* on March 19, 1929.

I have a husband and five children. I'm a weaver.... I get
paid by the day....

I get up at four to start breakfast for the children. When
you got five young 'uns it takes a while to dress 'em. The
oldest is nine and she helps a lot. The others are seven, five,
four, and three....

After I've got the children dressed and fed I take 'em to
the mill nursery, that is three of 'em. Two go to school, but
after school they go to the nursery until I get home from the
mill. The mill don't charge anythin' to keep the children
there. I couldn't afford it anyway. We have breakfast about
five, and I spend the rest of the time from five to seven gettin' the children ready and cleanin' up the house. That's about
the only time I get to clean up. Ruby washes the dishes.
Ruby is nine.

My husband and I go to the mill at seven. He's a stripper
in the cardin' room and gets $12.85 a week, but that's partly

From "How to Live on Forty-Six Cents a Day," by Paul Blanshard, *The Nation,* March
19, 1929. Reprinted with permission.

because they don't let him work Saturday mornin'. They put this stretch-out system on him shore enough. You know he's runnin' four jobs ever since they put this stretch-out system on him and he ain't gettin' any more than he used to get for one. Where'd they put the other three men?—why they laid 'em off and they give him the same $12.85 he got before.

I work in the weavin' room and I get $1.80 a day. That's $9.95 a week for five and a half days. I work from seven to six with an hour for dinner. I run up and down the alleys all day. No, they ain't no chance to sit down, except once in a long time when my work's caught up, but that's almost never.

At noon I run home and get dinner for the seven of us. The children come home from school and the nursery. . . . We have beans and baked sweets and bread and butter, and sometimes fat-back and sometimes pie, if I get time to bake it. Of course I make my own bread.

It takes about $16 a week to feed us. . . .

After dinner I wash the dishes and run back to the mill. We don't have any sink but there's a faucet with runnin' water on the back porch and a regular toilet there, too. . . .

Things Have Been Pretty Hard

When the whistle blows at six I come home and get supper. Then I put the children to bed. There's a double bed here and a double bed in that other room and a double bed out in the back room. That's for seven of us. The baby's pretty young. I 'spose all of the children'll go into the mills when they get a bit older. We'll need the money all right. Yes, my father and mother were mill workers, too, and they're still livin' and workin'. He gets $18 a week and my mother gets about $3 a week for workin' mornin's. . . . I went through the third grade in school and then I went to work in the mill. I was nine years old when I started work at Number 4 in Pelzer. My husband didn't go to school neither but he managed to pick up readin' and he reads books. Yes, we take a paper.

When supper is over I have a chance to make the children's clothes. Yes, I make 'em all, and all my own clothes, too. I never buy a dress at a store. I haven't no sewin' machine but I borrow the use of one. On Saturday night I wash the children in a big wash-tub and heat the water on the oil stove. Then I do the week's ironin'. I send the washin' to the laundry. I just couldn't do that, too. It costs nearly $2 a week. Our rent in this house is only $1.30 a week for the four rooms and we get water and electric lights free.

I always make a coat last seven or eight years. My husband gets a suit every two years but he ain't had one for the last six years. He got an overcoat about four years ago. Things have been pretty hard. . . .

No Rest

Maybe my children ought to get away from the mill village, but if they went anywhere they would go back to the farm and there ain't no use doin' that. The farmers haven't got it as good as we have. . . .

Sunday's about the only day I get to rest any. Seems as if I just have to have a little rest then.

Let's see, my babies cost $25 except the first one and that cost $30. 'Taint every doctor will do it for that. I never had any trouble. I worked up to two months before, mostly, an' I went back when the children was about four months old. The nursery'll take 'em when they're three weeks old. I had to hire a colored girl when the babies come. That cost $7 a week.

Birth control? What's that? . . . Oh! Sure, we'd be glad to have that if it didn't cost no money. . . .

Once I mashed my thumb in the mill. I was out for two months with it and I didn't get anythin'. I went to pull a loom and the handle on the lever slipped because the gear was too tight and it mashed my thumb. The company don't pay anythin' for a thing like that.

Usually I get to bed between ten and eleven at night.

Hard Times at the Ford Plant

Edmund Wilson

Throughout the twenties, more than one in eight adult Americans worked in the automobile industry, with almost 150,000 laboring at Ford's Rouge River plant in Detroit alone. Paying a wage of six dollars a day, Ford assembly line jobs were coveted by thousands of immigrants newly arrived in America. But as one English immigrant known only as Bert explains, life at the Ford plant was more like a nightmare than the American dream. He told his story to prolific author and social historian Edmund Wilson.

When I first came over [from England], I worked at Fisher Bodies for three months. I took a three-shift job on production at the start rather than be walkin' around. But then I went to Ford's—like everybody else, I'd 'eard about Ford's wages. And you do get the wages. I got $5 a day for the first two months and $6 ahfter, for a year or so—then I ashked for a raise and got forty cents more a day for two and a hahlf years—I never saw this $7 a day. But the wages are the only redeemin' feature. If he cut wages, they'd walk out on 'im. Ye get the wages, but ye sell your soul at Ford's—ye're worked like a slave all day, and when ye get out ye're too tired to do anything—ye go to sleep on the car comin' home. But as it is, once a Ford worker, always a Ford worker. Ye get lackadaisical, as they say in Lancashire—ye haven't got the guts to go. There's people who come to Ford's from the country, thinkin' they're goin' to make a little money—that they'll only work there a few years and then go back and be independent. And then they stay there forever—unless they get laid off. Ye've never got any security in your job. Finally they moved us out to the Rouge [River plant]—we were the first people down there—we pioneered there when the machinery wasn't hardly nailed down. But when they began gettin' ready for Model A, production shut down and we were out of a job. I'd tried to get transferred, but they laid me off. Then I 'eard they were wantin' some die-makers—I'd never worked at die-makin', but I said I'd 'ad five years at it and got a job, and I was in that department three years till I got laid off last July. I ashked to be transferred and they laid me off. They'll lay ye off now for any reason or no reason.

You Never Know Where You're At

It's worse than the army, I tell ye—ye're badgered and victimized all the time. You get wise to the army after a while, but at Ford's ye never know where ye're at. One day ye can go down the aisle and the next day they'll tell ye to get the hell out of it. In one department, they'll ashk ye why the hell ye haven't got gloves on and in another why the hell ye're wearin' them. If ye're wearin' a clean apron, they'll throw oil on it, and if a machinist takes pride in 'is tools, they'll throw 'em on the floor while he's out. The bosses are thick as treacle and they're always on your neck, because the man above is on their neck and Sorenson's on the neck of the whole lot—he's the man that pours the boiling oil down that old Henry makes. There's a man born a hundred years too late, a regular slave driver—the men tremble when they see Sorenson comin'. He used to be very brutal—he'd come through and slug the men. One day when they were movin' the plant he came through and found a man sittin' workin' on a box. "Get up!" says Sorenson. "Don't ye know ye can't sit down in here?" The man never moved and Sorenson kicked the box out from under 'im—and the man got up and bashed Sorenson one in the jaw. "Go to hell!" he says. "I don't work here—I'm workin' for the Edison Company!"

Then ye only get fifteen minutes for lunch. The lunch wagon comes around—the ptomaine wagon, we call it. Ye pay fifteen cents for a damn big pile o' sawdust. And they let you buy some wonderful water that hasn't seen milk for a month. Sorenson owns stock in one of the lunch companies, I'm told. A man's food is in 'is neck when he starts workin'—it 'asn't got time to reach 'is stomach.

A man checks 'is brains and 'is freedom at the door when he goes to work at Ford's. Some of those [immigrants] with their feet wet and no soles to their shoes are glad to get under a dry roof—but not for me! I'm tryin' to forget about it.

The Attorney General Denounces "Reds"

A. Mitchell Palmer

In the 1920s, poorly paid workers who tried to organize for better conditions were often branded as communists. Many of these working people were recent immigrants to the United States. Playing on the unfounded fears of millions of Americans, powerful U.S. attorney general A. Mitchell Palmer achieved political notoriety rounding up and deporting thousands of suspected communist sympathizers during the early years of the decade. In the excerpt below, Palmer defends his actions with harsh words for immigrants, union organizers, socialists, and others who were perceived to be sympathetic to the communist cause.

Although his actions were judged unconstitutional, Palmer was cleared of charges brought against him and he retired from public life in 1921 at the end of President Woodrow Wilson's term in office.

I n this brief review of the work which the Department of Justice has undertaken, to tear out the radical seeds that have entangled American ideas in their poisonous theories, I desire not merely to explain what the real menace of communism is, but also to tell how we have been compelled to clean up the country almost unaided by any virile legislation. Though I have not been embarrassed by political opposition, I have been materially delayed because the present

From "The Case Against the 'Reds,'" by A. Mitchell Palmer, *Forum,* vol. 63 (February 1920).

sweeping processes of arrests and deportation of seditious aliens should have been vigorously pushed by Congress last spring [in 1919]. . . .

The anxiety of that period . . . when Congress, ignoring the seriousness of these vast organizations that were plotting to overthrow the Government, failed to act, has passed. The time came when it was obviously hopeless to expect the hearty co-operation of Congress, in the only way to stamp out these seditious societies in their open defiance of law by various forms of propaganda.

The Blaze of Revolution

Like a prairie-fire, the blaze of revolution was sweeping over every American institution of law and order a year ago. It was eating its way into the homes of the American workman, its sharp tongues of revolutionary heat were licking the altars of the churches, leaping into the belfry of the school bell, crawling into the sacred corners of American homes, seeking to replace marriage vows with libertine laws, burning up the foundations of society.

Robbery, not war, is the ideal of communism. This has been demonstrated in Russia, Germany, and in America. As a foe, the anarchist is fearless of his own life, for his creed is a fanaticism that admits no respect of any other creed. Obviously it is the creed of any criminal mind, which reasons always from motives impossible to clean thought. Crime is the degenerate factor in society.

Upon these two basic certainties, first that the "Reds" were criminal aliens, and secondly that the American Government must prevent crime, it was decided that there could be no nice distinctions drawn between the theoretical ideals of the radicals and their actual violations of our national laws. An assassin may have brilliant intellectuality, he may be able to excuse his murder or robbery with fine oratory, but any theory which excuses crime is not wanted in America. This is no place for the criminal to flourish, nor will he do so, so long as the rights of common citizenship can be exerted to prevent him.

Our Government in Jeopardy

It has always been plain to me that when American citizens unite upon any national issue, they are generally right, but it is sometimes difficult to make the issue clear to them. If the Department of Justice could succeed in attracting the attention of our optimistic citizens to the issue of internal revolution in this country, we felt sure there would be no revolution. The Government was in jeopardy. My private in-

An Innocent Victim of Intolerance

The majority of immigrants nabbed in Attorney General A. Mitchell Palmer's Red Scare raids were simply practicing their right to free speech and free assembly as guaranteed in the Constitution. Few if any advocated overthrowing the government. In the excerpt below, a Russian immigrant named Semeon Nakhwat explains the pain he suffered simply for belonging to a Russian social organization.

I was born in Grodno, Russia, and am thirty-three years old and unmarried.

In the autumn of 1919, I was a member of the Union of Russian Workers. I am not an anarchist, Socialist or Bolshevik and do not take much interest in political theories. I joined the Russian Workers because I was a workman speaking Russian and wanted to associate with other Russians and have the benefit of the social intercourse and instruction in mechanics which the society gave. By trade I am a machinist.

On November 8, 1919, I was at a meeting of Russians in Bridgeport, who had come together to discuss ways and means for buying an automobile to be used for instruction purposes. . . . I was arrested with all the other men at the meeting, 63 in number. . . . No warrant of arrest was shown me then or at any other time, nor did I see any warrant shown to anyone else who was arrested.

I was taken with the other men to the police station . . . and held there three days, being in a cell with two other men.

formation of what was being done by the organization known as the Communist Party of America, with headquarters in Chicago, of what was being done by the Communist Internationale under their manifesto planned at Moscow last March . . . addressed "To the Proletariats [workers] of All Countries," of what strides the Communist Labor Party was making, removed all doubt. In this conclusion we did not ignore the definite standards of personal liberty, of free speech, which is the very temperament and heart of the

During these three days no one gave me any hearing or asked me any questions. . . .

I was held in the Hartford Jail for six weeks without any hearing. In the seventh week I had one hearing before the Labor Department, which hearing was held in the Post Office Building and was then returned to jail.

In the thirteenth week of my confinement [government agent] Edward J. Hickey came into my cell and asked me to give him the address of a man called Boyko in Greenpoint, Brooklyn. I did not know this man and told Hickey that I did not. Hickey thereupon struck me twice with his fist, once in the forehead and once in the jaw, whereupon I fell. He then kicked me and I became unconscious. Hickey is a big man, weighing two hundred pounds. . . .

I was released from the Hartford Jail on April 7th, having been in confinement five months, my release coming about through an attorney who came to the jail to see other prisoners and who, after seeing me, obtained a reduction of my bail from ten thousand dollars to one thousand dollars, and secured the putting up of $1,000 bail. . . .

Since my release on the 7th day of April I have been unable to secure employment, being informed wherever I apply and state my record that persons under suspicion of being bolsheviks are not desired. I have made diligent effort to obtain employment but have been unable to do so.

Semeon Nakhwat in *The Social Setting of Intolerance*. Glenview, IL: Scott, Foresman and Company, 1964.

people. The evidence was examined with the utmost care, with a personal leaning toward freedom of thought and word on all questions.

The whole mass of evidence, accumulated from all parts of the country, was scrupulously scanned, not merely for the written or spoken differences of viewpoint as to the Government of the United States, but, in spite of these things, to see if the hostile declarations might not be sincere in their announced motive to improve our social order. There was no hope of such a thing.

By stealing, murder and lies, Bolshevism [communism] has looted Russia not only of its material strength, but of its moral force. A small clique of outcasts from the East Side of New York has attempted this, with what success we all know. Because a disreputable alien—[Russian revolutionary] Leon Bronstein, the man who now calls himself Trotzky—can inaugurate a reign of terror from his throne room in the Kremlin; because this lowest of all types known to New York can sleep in the Czar's bed, while hundreds of thousands in Russia are without food or shelter, should Americans be swayed by such doctrines?

Such a question, it would seem, should receive but one answer from America. . . .

Will Deportations Check Bolshevism?

Behind, and underneath, my own determination to drive from our midst the agents of Bolshevism with increasing vigor and with greater speed, until there are no more of them left among us, so long as I have the responsible duty of that task, I have discovered the hysterical methods of these revolutionary humans with increasing amazement and suspicion. In the confused information that sometimes reaches the people, they are compelled to ask questions which involve the reasons for my acts against the "Reds." I have been asked, for instance, to what extent deportation will check radicalism in this country. Why not ask what will become of the United States Government if these alien radicals are permitted to carry out the principles of the

Communist Party as embodied in its so-called laws, aims and regulations?

There wouldn't be any such thing left. In place of the United States Government we should have the horror and terrorism of bolsheviki tyranny such as is destroying Russia now. Every scrap of radical literature demands the overthrow of our existing government. All of it demands obedience to the instincts of criminal minds, that is, to the lower appetites, mate-rial and moral. The whole purpose of communism appears to be a mass formation of the criminals of the world to overthrow the decencies of private life, to usurp property that they have not earned, to disrupt the present order of life regardless of health, sex or religious rights. By a literature that promises the wildest dreams of such low aspirations, that can occur to only the criminal minds, communism distorts our social law.

The chief appeal communism makes is to "The Worker." If they can lure the wage-earner to join their own gang of thieves, if they can show him that he will be rich if he steals, so far they have succeeded in betraying him to their own criminal course. . . .

Conquer and Destroy

[The communist] manifesto further embraces the various organizations in this country of men and women obsessed with discontent, having disorganized relations to American society. These include the I.W.W.'s [International Workers of the World], the most radical socialists, the misguided anarchists, the agitators who oppose the limitations of unionism, the moral perverts and the hysterical women who abound in communism. . . .

Naturally the Communist Party has bored its revolutionary points into the Socialist Party. They managed to split the Socialists, for the so-called Left Wing of the Socialist Party is now the Communist Party, which specifically states that it does not intend to capture the bourgeoisie parliamentary state, but to conquer and destroy, and that the final objective, mass action, is the medium intended to be used in the conquest and destruction of the bourgeoisie state to annihilate the parliamentary state, and introduce a revolutionary dictatorship of the Proletariat. . . .

There is no legislation at present which can reach an American citizen who is discontented with our system of American Government, nor is it necessary. . . .

The first congress of the Communist Nationale held March 6, 1919, in Moscow, subscribed to by Trotzky . . . adopted the following:

This makes necessary the disarming of the bourgeoisie at the proper time, the arming of the laborer, and the formation of a communist army as the protectors of the rules of the proletariat and the inviolability of the social structure.

When we realize that each member of the Communist Party of America pledges himself to the principles above set forth, deportation of men and women bound to such a theory is a very mild reformatory sentence. . . .

It is my belief that while they have stirred discontent in our midst, while they have caused irritating strikes, and while they have infected our social ideas with the disease of their own minds and their unclean morals, we can get rid of them! and not until we have done so shall we have removed the menace of Bolshevism for good.

The Ku Klux Klan Takes Indiana

William E. Wilson

By the 1920s, the Ku Klux Klan had more than 4 million members who exercised great political power in many states, including Indiana, which was said to have the most powerful Klan. Author William E. Wilson was a college freshman in 1924, when his father, an Indiana congressman, ran head-on into the political power of the Klan and lost his seat in the House. That same year, the Klan elected Edward Jackson for Indiana's governor. In the following excerpt, Wilson describes the fear, anger, and hatred during that long, hot summer when the Klan was riding high across the Indiana countryside.

W hen I think of the nineteen twenties, I think of the heat of summers in southern Indiana where I spent my vacations from Harvard. They were mostly happy summers, but there was one that was not—the summer of 1924, which came at the end of my freshman year. It glows luridly in my memory, an ordeal by fire through which I had to pass in the process of growing up.

We drove home to Evansville that year from Washington, D.C., in mid-June, my father and mother and sister and I, in the family Hudson. I had taken the Federal Express [train] down from Boston as soon as my exams were over, and the next day we left the capital, where my father had just finished his first term as a congressman from Indiana. I was pleased with myself, secretly but no doubt obviously, for

Excerpted from "Long, Hot Summer in Indiana," by William E. Wilson, *American Heritage*, August 1965. Reprinted by permission of American Heritage Inc.

surviving the year at Harvard fresh and green out of a mid-western high school, and I was proud of my father for *his* record as a freshman in Congress. . . .

On our arrival in Evansville, there was the old house on Chandler Avenue to explore and readjust to. . . . There were also those first home-cooked meals after a year of institutional fare, and there was the impatient waiting, all that long first day, to see an old high-school friend whom I shall call Link Patterson. Link had not gone to college and had a job, like any grown man; he would not be at home till suppertime.

Not the Same Person

After supper I walked over to Link's house. . . . But the Link Patterson who met me on his front porch that night was not the Link Patterson I remembered. He looked the same and he greeted me in the old way, by cracking me hard on the biceps with his fist as I came up the porch steps. But he was not the old Link Patterson. Nor were his parents the same. I had loved his mother almost as much as I loved my own, and his father—garrulous, bawdy, and uninhibited—had always given me a man-to-man feeling that I had never shared with my own more dignified father. But that night Mrs. Patterson was restrained and formal and seemed only half-glad to see me, and Mr. Patterson said almost nothing at all. I remember especially how they watched me, as if they were waiting to accuse me of something that they knew about but I did not.

The four of us sat on Link's porch for a while exchanging banalities. . . . At the end of a half hour, Link said, "I'm sorry, Bill, but Mom and Dad and I have to be somewhere at eight o'clock," and I left and walked home, disappointed and puzzled.

My sister said I had outgrown Link Patterson, and that made me angry because it implied that I had become a snob or something. But my mother said it was sometimes hard to renew an old acquaintance, and she was sure Link and I would be back on the old basis soon. My father said nothing. He sat in the porch swing drumming his fingers on the arm of it in the way that made my mother nervous, until my mother finally said, "Will, I wish you wouldn't do that," and he got up and said he had to go down to the office, and wouldn't I like to come along?

We drove down Chandler to Fourth and down Fourth toward Main. As we approached a large vacant lot we saw that a crowd was gathered under floodlights, and a fiddlers' contest was in progress on a platform in the blue haze of a pit barbecue. My father said, "That's probably where the Pattersons are tonight. The Agoga Bible Class is raising money to build a tabernacle on that lot. They outgrew the Strand Theatre and moved into the Victory Theatre, and now they've outgrown it. They gave the preacher an automobile last month."

"But the Pattersons aren't Baptists," I said.

"Those aren't all Baptists, by any means," my father said, gesturing toward the crowd as we passed. "There aren't that many Baptists in Vanderburgh County."

"Aren't you going to stop?" I asked, remembering the church socials we had attended during his campaign two years before, when I had eaten chicken and dumplings of every Christian denomination.

My father shook his head.

"I'm afraid it wouldn't do any good. Harry Rowbottom has priority in that crowd." Harry Rowbottom was my father's Republican opponent. He had come to Evansville from Cincinnati eleven years before, had worked as a clerk in an oil company, and served three terms in the Indiana House of Representatives. He was not yet forty that summer, fourteen years younger than my father. I had never seen him, and I would not have a glimpse of him in his public life until 1928, when I was a newspaper reporter in Evansville. From that later period I remember him as a bombastic and platitudinous speaker, a vigorous man with large bovine eyes set wide apart in a heavy dark face. . . .

"Join the Klan, or Else!"

He parked the car on Main Street and went into his office, leaving me alone to ponder his irritation about the Bible class barbecue. He was a man who seldom lost his temper. When he returned to the car, he did not start the motor but sat in silence for a minute or two watching the Saturday-night shoppers pass on the sidewalk. Finally, without preface, he said: "Son, I'm not going to be re-elected in the fall."

"You're joking," I said.

He shook his head.

"A lot of people have turned against me," he said, "a lot of good, honest, but misguided people like your friends the Pattersons. I decided I'd better tell you tonight, before you begin to hear it from others."

"Why, Dad, you can't help winning!" I said. "As many Republicans vote for you as Democrats. You've always said that yourself. And there are all those things you've done in your first term—the Ohio River bridge and the tax bill you wrote with Mr. Garner and—"

"It isn't what I've done that counts," he said. "It's what I have refused to do."

"What is that?"

"Join the Ku Klux Klan."

In Cambridge I had read newspaper stories about the Ku Klux Klan that was being revived from the ashes of [the] old Klan of Reconstruction days. . . . I did not take the modern Klan seriously.

"But of course!" I said. "A man like you isn't going to dress up in a sheet and make a fool of himself!"

Father shook his head again.

"It's a very serious matter out here this year," he said. "Senator [Samuel Moffett] Ralston warned me about it when he came back from a trip to Indiana last Christmas, and when I came out here in the spring for the primary, I was told to join the Klan, *or else*. I refused, of course, and now they're out to beat me, if they have to steal votes to do it. Your mother and sister don't know yet. I wish I could send them away during the campaign, but of course your mother wouldn't leave me in an election year. This summer is going to be an ugly business, son. I wish there were some way I could spare all three of you." . . .

"Those people know your worth," I said, nodding toward the crowds passing on the sidewalk, "and they will vote for you."

"Too many of them have been bamboozled into a sense of self-righteousness by a bunch of demagogues," he said. "We've gone a long way in this country, but apparently we still haven't freed men and women of their suspicion of each other, their prejudices, their intolerance. I think that is going to be the big battle of this century. My little fight here in Indiana is just a preliminary skirmish and my practical political sense tells me I'm going to lose it. I'm not a crusader by nature, but, God help me, I'm not going to budge one inch from where I stand!". . .

"I Am the Law"

On Monday, still incredulous, I went out to the Willard Library on the other side of town and did some long-neglected homework among the bound newspapers on the political situation in Indiana.

There was a man named D.C. Stephenson who had come to Evansville from Texas two years before and entered the Democratic primary but, without explanation, had not campaigned and had lost the nomination to my father by an overwhelming majority. D.C. Stephenson was now, in 1924, Grand Dragon of the Ku Klux Klan in Indiana, which had a half million members, and he was ruling his Invisible Empire from a luxurious suite of offices in Indianapolis. "I am the law in Indiana," he was saying. Although he was only thirty-three years old, he signed his letters "The Old Man." In April 1924, Governor Warren T. McCray had been sentenced to federal prison for using the mails to defraud, and Stephenson was supporting McCray's secretary of state, Ed Jackson, as the Republican candidate to succeed him. Jackson had given the Ku Klux Klan its charter to organize in Indiana three years before, and Stephenson had become the organizer in 1922. . . . Rumor had it that Stephenson had made over two million dollars in eighteen months from the sale of Klan memberships and Klan regalia. A congressman's salary in those years was only $7,500.

Stephenson was also supporting my father's Republican opponent now. But whether men like Harry Rowbottom and Ed Jackson on the Klan slate were actual members of the Klan was a question that could not be answered, for in 1924 no one except Klan officials was publicly professing membership. After all, candidates for office did not have to make an issue of the Klan; the Klan's support was enough. In the spring of 1924, Stephenson was quoted in the newspapers as saying, "God help the man who issues a declaration of war against the Klan in Indiana now." This meant any man, like my father, who refused to go along with their intolerance.

The times were ripe for the Klan's views in the mid-Twenties. [After World War I, President] Woodrow Wilson's internationalism had been repudiated; provincialism was the order of the day. Corruption had been the order of the day during the [Warren G.] Harding administration, and his successor [Calvin Coolidge] was the apostle of mediocrity. . . . America was in the doldrums of a vulgar prosperity from which any kind of "crusade" would be a relief. White Protestant Americanism was the "ideal" the Ku Klux Klan set up for the smug and self-righteous who shared in the nation's prosperity and for the malcontents who had no share in it. If you were rich you could attribute your riches to your God-given right as a one-hundred-per-cent American to be rich and to be suspicious of anyone not of your kind who wanted to share the wealth with you; if you were not rich, you could at least be proud that you were not a Catholic who worshipped in Latin, a Jew who had a foreign-sounding name, or a Negro whose skin was black. Complacency and boredom, combined with an unacknowledged sense of guilt, can demoralize a nation as much as division or dissension.

"Politics Is Different"

Although I had promised my parents to take some vacation before I looked for a summer job, I set out from the library at once to find one. I wanted to return to college in the fall, but I knew that my father, out of office, was going to have a hard time keeping me there. Within an hour I was signed up to work for the Crescent City Refining Company in one of their filling stations. I was to work weeknights from five o'clock to nine, with one night off, and twelve-hour shifts on Saturdays and Sundays, and my pay would be fifteen dollars a week. That was not much toward a Harvard education, even in those days, but it was something. I went to work that evening.

I had been assigned to a station at the edge of the Negro district, and at quarter to five I appeared for work in oversized khaki coveralls that my father wore when he tinkered with the Hudson.

"I'm the new helper," I said to the man who sat in a chair tilted against the one shaded wall in the sun-beaten waste of the station. "Schelhaus" is as close as I can come to remembering his name.

He looked me up and down slowly, chewing on a matchstick. A long, oily nose drooped over his thin mouth. His black eyes were set close together. Finally he dropped the front legs of the chair sharply to the concrete.

"College boy, ain't you?"

"Yes, sir."

"What's your name?"

"Bill Wilson."

"Wilson? You the Congressman's son?"

"Yes, sir."

"I heard they hired a couple of boys today and you was one of 'em." He looked at the hand he had raised from a grease-stained knee. The hand was wrinkled, oily, and brown. He studied it uncertainly for a moment and then let it drop back upon the knee. "Well, you're on time. That's something. Name's Schelhaus. You take your orders from me."

"They told me downtown that you were the boss here, Mr. Schelhaus," I said.

"You're goddam right I am!"

At that moment another man came round a corner of the station, and Schelhaus said, "Here's the new helper, Dave.

We got the Congressman's son." He stood up then, went inside, and shut himself in the toilet.

Dave looked friendlier than Schelhaus. He was younger, thirty maybe, with a wide mouth and yellow hair and blue eyes. He kept taking off his cap and putting it back on, like a baseball player.

"Schelhaus is an s.o.b., kid," he said. "You 'n' me'll stick together."

"Apparently he doesn't like my father's politics," I said. "Or maybe it's because I'm a college student."

Dave took off his cap and put it back on.

"Are you a crossback, kid?"

"A what?" I said.

"Catholic."

"No," I said. "Why?"

"I heard your old man was one."

"Well, he isn't," I said. "But what difference would it make if he was?"

"We don't want no crossbacks or kikes around here," Dave said. "Politics is different. Nobody's a Democrat or Republican any more. Hell, I used to be a Democrat myself! And you being a college boy is O.K.—with me anyhow. I wouldn't've minded going to college myself." . . .

"If It's a Free Country . . . "

The first Negro came into the station about an hour after I started working. He was driving a Ford truck, with "Hauling" painted crudely on the panels. I wiped the windshield and filled the radiator while Dave stood at the back cranking out the gasoline. It was not until the truck drove off that I saw the dark, rainbow-streaked puddle of gasoline on the concrete. Dave must have spilled at least a gallon. I was sure that before long Schelhaus would lash out at him for his carelessness, and there was an awkward silence among us when I sat down between him and Dave and tilted my chair against the wall.

"What the hell did you mean, doing that?" Schelhaus said, finally.

I glanced covertly at Dave, who remained silent, his gaze fixed on the cars passing in the street.

"You a Bolshevik [communist] or something?" Schelhaus said.

Still Dave did not speak, and then I saw that Schelhaus was addressing me.

"You mean me?"

"Who the hell else would I mean? What did you think you were doing back there?" . . .

I turned in appeal to Dave. But Dave continued to stare straight ahead.

"I don't know what you mean," I said.

"Oh, yes, you do!" Schelhaus said. "You know damn well what I mean. Giving that nigger radiator service and wiping off his windshield."

"But you said—"

"I never said you was to give free service to a goddam black nigger!" Schelhaus shouted, sweat popping out on his oily forehead. "There ain't no job in this country can make a white man wait on a nigger! This is still a free country, and you'd better learn that pretty quick—you and your old man both!"

At the unexpected inclusion of my father in the tirade, I lost my temper.

"If it's a free country, then the Negro should get the same service as everybody else," I said.

"The *Nee*gro!" Schelhaus mocked, almost screaming. "Listen to him, will you? The *Nee*gro!"

Before I could speak again, he got up and went into the toilet and slammed the door behind him. . . .

Although neither Schelhaus nor Dave ever came right out and admitted being a Klansman, both revealed their prejudices more openly than most people did. On the subject of the Ku Klux Klan a strange silence prevailed everywhere that summer, and you could not be sure whether your friends were members of the Invisible Empire or not. Those who were not members were afraid to talk, I suppose; and those who were members were instructed to make a mystery of the organization.

In the main, the politicians too were silent. Those who had the endorsement of the Klan accepted it without comment. Coolidge himself, for example, never repudiated the Klan, never so much as publicly acknowledged its existence. Those who were opposed by the Klan were never sure exactly where, what, or whom to attack because of the general anonymity of their enemies. John W. Davis, when the Democrats finally nominated him for President after 103 ballots that summer, issued a denunciation of the Klan, and the Democratic candidate for governor of Indiana, Dr. Carleton B. McCulloch, said: "The Republican Party has been captured by the Ku Klux Klan and has, as a political party, for the present ceased to exist in Indiana." But such denunciations and remarks were ignored by the Republicans, and the opponents of the Klan, among them my father, found themselves boxing with shadows. As for the people who would do the voting in November, they simply weren't talking.

The Horse Thief Detective Association

My summer wasn't all misery. . . . I found a new girl . . . and for a while we thought we were in love, but I never learned where she or her family stood on the issue of the Klan. She would not talk about it. Almost every time I took her out, my car was trailed by the Horse Thief Detective Association, which was the police force of the Klan. It was always the same car that did the trailing, and I finally got used to it. It would pick me up about a block from our house, follow me to my girl's house, and wait while I went in to get her, and then follow us to the movies or wherever we were going. When we came out, it was there waiting and would follow us home. One night, when I eluded its shadow and parked on a country road with her, a farmer pulled up beside us and said, "If you kids know what is good for you, you'll move along. The Kluxers are patrolling this road tonight, and God knows what they'll do to you if they catch you here."

I knew. At least I had read and heard stories of what the Horse Thief Detective Association was doing to others. They entered homes without search warrants and flogged errant

Local Ku Klux Klan groups, which frequently included respected members of the community, often threatened citizens who opposed them or refused to join their ranks.

husbands and wives. They tarred and feathered drunks. They raided stills and burned barns. They caught couples in parked cars and tried to blackmail the girls, or worse. On occasion, they branded the three K's on the bodies of people who were particularly offensive to them. And over in Illinois there had even been a couple of murders. I took my girl home.

No violence befell me or anyone in my family that summer. Not even a fiery cross was burned in our yard, although I saw crosses burning on hillsides near the places where my father spoke. But there was always the threat of violence around us in the hot and humid air of those breathless months. By chance I answered a number of the anonymous telephone calls we got at our house. "Hi, nigger-lover," the calls often began, and thereafter were so obscene they were unprintable. I am sure that my father got plenty of them, at his office and at home. Contrary to his former custom of sitting unmoved beside a ringing telephone and letting someone else in the family answer it, he always leaped toward it ahead of the rest of us that summer. Often he hung up without a word and returned to his chair. "Wrong number," he would say, if we asked him who it was. I suppose my mother answered some of those calls too, and my sister. But we never mentioned them in the family.

There were also anonymous letters in my father's mail— threats, innuendoes, scurrilous abuse, obscenities. He never spoke of them, but years later, after he died, I found a collection of them shoved into the back of his safe-deposit box at the bank. I don't know why he kept them. Maybe he forgot they were there. A couple were informing letters which, if he had chosen to use them, might have ruined some of his political enemies.

There were continual petty annoyances, pranks mostly, not intended to do us any harm but designed to create an atmosphere of anxiety and dread. More than once, when Father was at a meeting or when I had a date, the air was let out of the Hudson's tires or the battery was disconnected. Our window screens were soaped with the three K's. In the middle of the night the telephone would ring and when we answered, no one would be there. One sneak enjoyed a particularly annoying practice of partially unscrewing the light bulbs in our garage, so that when we drove in at night we could not turn them on. . . .

The Rise and Fall

As July wore on into the dog days of August, the Klan came more into the open—as an organization that is. . . .

Klantauguas, or lectures on the principles of the Ku Klux Klan, were common at club meetings and semipublic gatherings. Processions of robed Klansmen marched into churches on Sunday mornings in the middle of services and laid sums of money on offertory rails, and some preachers were suborned and spoke in support of "the Klan ideal" thereafter. One who did not, in the northern part of the state, was taken across the Michigan line and branded. The Klan licensed bootleggers, and the Horse Thief Detective Association raided those who did not pay. Kiddy Klaverns were organized, Konsorts gathered in auxiliary clubs, and an abortive plan was launched to make Valparaiso University, upstate, into a Klan Kollege. The Klan's *Kourier* solicited the membership of native-born, white, Protestant Hoosiers and offered Klectokons, the Klan regalia, for sale. . . .

Power eventually corrupted the efficiency of the Klan, and the leaders began to quarrel among themselves. D.C. Stephenson broke with the national leader, Hiram Wesley Evans, early in his bid for power, and in time was himself being "banished" by local Klaverns here and there in Indiana over various disputes. But he remained "the law" in our state until April 2, 1925, when he was arrested for sadistic sexual assault on a young Indianapolis woman named Madge Oberholtzer. Twelve days later Madge Oberholtzer died, and the charge was changed to murder. According to the young woman's dying statement, Stephenson and two henchmen kidnapped her and took her to a town in northern Indiana. Stephenson, she said, had viciously assaulted her on the train en route; then he held her prisoner in a hotel. Finally, to console her, he sent her out with money to buy a new hat. She bought poison instead, and when Stephenson discovered she had taken it, he refused to call a doctor and drove her home to Indianapolis and dumped her on her doorstep. Stephenson always protested that he was "framed" by his enemies, but he was sentenced to life imprisonment for second-degree murder.

Black Fundamentalism in Harlem

Marcus Garvey

The economic boom of the twenties did very little to improve the lives of most black people in the United States. To counter the effects of grinding poverty and racism, West Indian immigrant Marcus Garvey started the United Negro Improvement Association (UNIA) in the Harlem neighborhood of New York City. Through his speeches and newspaper *Negro World,* Garvey taught black nationalism and black pride and urged African Americans to study their own culture and to find heroes among members of their own race.

Garvey was accused by the U.S. government of using illegal methods to raise funds for UNIA, and imprisoned for mail fraud in 1925. He was immediately deported to Jamaica upon his release in 1927. There he continued to speak out on the rights of black people. The following excerpts are typical of Garvey's speeches during the late 1920s.

Speech I: African Fundamentalism

Fellow Men of the Negro Race, Greeting:
   The time has come for the Negro to forget and cast behind him his hero worship and adoration of other races, and to start out immediately, to create and emulate heroes of his own.

We must canonize our own saints, create our own martyrs, and elevate to positions of fame and honor black men and women who have made their distinct contributions to our racial history. [Former slave and abolitionist] Sojourner Truth is worthy of the place of sainthood alongside of Joan of Arc; Crispus Attucks [killed in the Boston Massacre] . . . [is] entitled to the halo of martyrdom with no less glory than that of the martyrs of any other race. [Nineteenth-century leader of Haitian independence] Toussaint L'Ouverture's brilliancy as a soldier and statesman outshone that of a Cromwell, Napoleon and Washington; hence, he is entitled to the highest place as a hero among men. Africa has produced countless numbers of men and women, in war and in peace, whose lustre and bravery outshine that of any other people. Then why not see good and perfection in ourselves?

The Right to Our Doctrine

We must inspire a literature and promulgate a doctrine of our own without any apologies to the powers that be. The right is ours and God's. Let contrary sentiment and cross opinions go to the winds. Opposition to race independence is the weapon of the enemy to defeat the hopes of an unfortunate people. We are entitled to our own opinions and not obligated to or bound by the opinions of others.

If others laugh at you, return the laughter to them; if they mimic you, return the compliment with equal force. They have no more right to dishonor, disrespect and disregard your feeling and manhood than you have in dealing with them. Honor them when they honor you; disrespect and disregard them when they vilely treat you. Their arrogance is but skin deep and an assumption that has no foundation in morals or in law. They have sprung from the same family tree of obscurity as we have; their history is as rude in its primitiveness as ours; their ancestors ran wild and naked, lived in caves and in the branches of trees, like monkeys, as ours; they made human sacrifices, ate the flesh of their own dead and the raw meat of the wild beast for centuries even

as they accuse us of doing; their cannibalism was more pro-
longed than ours; when we were embracing the arts and
sciences on the banks of the Nile their ancestors were still
drinking human blood and eating out of the skulls of their
conquered dead; when our civilization had reached the
noonday of progress they were still running naked and
sleeping in holes and caves with rats, bats and other insects
and animals. After we had already unfathomed the mysteries of the stars and reduced the heavenly constellations to
minute and regular calculus they were still backwoodsmen,
living in ignorance and blatant darkness.

Why Be Discouraged?

The world today is indebted to us for the benefits of civilization. They stole our arts and sciences from Africa. Then
why should we be ashamed of ourselves? Their *modern im-
provements* are but *duplicates* of a grander civilization that
we reflected thousands of years ago, without the advantage
of what is buried and still hidden, to be resurrected and rein-
troduced by the intelligence of our generation and our prosperity. Why should we be discouraged because somebody
laughs at us today? Who's to tell what tomorrow will bring
forth? Did they not laugh at Moses, Christ and Mohammed?
Was there not a Carthage, Greece and Rome? We see and
have changes every day, so pray, work, be steadfast and be
not dismayed.

As the Jew is held together by his *religion,* the white
races by the assumption and the unwritten law of *superiority,* and the Mongolian by the precious tie of *blood,* so likewise the Negro must be united in one *grand racial hierarchy. Our union must know no clime, boundary*, or
nationality. Like the great Church of Rome, Negroes the
world over *must practice one faith,* that of Confidence in
themselves, with One God! One Aim! One Destiny! Let no
religious scruples, no political machination divide us, but
let us hold together under all climes and in every country,
making among ourselves a Racial Empire upon which "the
sun shall never set."

Allegiance to Self First

Let no voice but your own speak to you from the depths. Let no influence but your own raise you in time of peace and time of war. Hear all, but attend only that which concerns you.

Your first allegiance shall be to your God, then to your family, race and country. Remember always that the Jew in his political and economic urge is always first a Jew; the white man is first a white man under all circumstances, and you can do no less than being first and always a Negro, and then all else will take care of itself. Let no one inoculate you for their own conveniences. There is no humanity before that which starts with yourself. "Charity begins at home." First to thyself be true, and "thou canst not then be false to any man."

God and Nature first made us what we are, and then out of our own creative genius we make ourselves what we want to be. Follow always that great law.

Let the sky and God be our limit, and Eternity our measurement. There is no height to which we cannot climb by using the active intelligence of our own minds. Mind creates, and as much as we desire in Nature we can have through the creation of our own minds. Being at present the scientifically weaker race, you shall treat others only as they treat you; but in your homes and everywhere possible you must teach the higher development of science to your children; and be sure to develop a race of scientists par excellence, for in science and religion lies our only hope to withstand the evil designs of modern materialism. Never forget your God. Remember, we live, work and pray for the establishing of a great and binding *racial hierarchy,* the founding of a *racial empire* whose only natural, spiritual and political limits shall be God and "Africa, at home and abroad." . . .

Speech II: Fount of Inspiration

I am going to speak to you from the thoughts contained in [the speech] *"African Fundamentalism,"* so that they may be advised, I expected every Negro home at this time to secure a copy of this Creed for the guidance of the Race.

Tonight I will speak from the first sentence of *"African Fundamentalism"*—*"The time has come for the Negro to forget and cast behind him his hero worship and adoration of other races, and to start out immediately to create and emulate heroes of his own."*

Any race that accepts the thoughts of another race, automatical[l]y, becomes the slave race of that other race. As men think, so they do react above the things around them. When men are taught to think in a certain groove they act similarly. It is no wonder that the Negro acts so peculiarly within our present civilization, because he has been trained and taught to accept the thoughts of a race that has made itself by assumption superior. The Negro during the time of slavery accepted his thoughts and opinions from the white race, by so doing he admitted into his system the idea of the superiority of a master in relationship to a slave. In one instance he was freed, that is, from chattel slav[e]ry; but up to the time of the Universal Negro Improvement Association, he was not free in mind. "African Fundamentalism" seeks to emancipate the Negro from the thoughts of others who are encouraging him to act on [their?] opinions and thoughts. Any [race?] that has succeeded in the world— speaking of the ancient world up to the present world, will tell you that they succeeded by thinking and acting for themselves. Whether they be the Meads [Medes] or the Persians, the Greeks or the Romans, the English or the Americans, each and everyone, ancient and modern, will tell you that their ability to rise above others and to establish themselves in the world was only made possible through the fact that they thought and acted for themselves. And we who have studied the trend of world events, seriously recommend to the Negro that he can only do this when he starts to think and act for himself. He must create around him his own philosophy—the semblance of everything that he desires for himself. That is what *"African Fundamentalism"* seeks to do,—establish a creed, as a guide, so that you will make few mistakes, if any, in the world. Because if you act on the thoughts of others, so long will they remain your superiors;

for no man is so just, because of the sins of the world, to treat his brother as he would that others treat him. Man will not treat his brother with equity. We have one race pulling against the other, so that it has almost become an axiom. "That no man will think equally for his brother," and so those who have imposed their thoughts upon you, will give you only that thought to let you serve them as slaves.

Create Our Own Heroes

To emancipate yourselves from that you must accept something original, something racially your own, and that is what we want you the Negroes, . . . to do—accept a Philosophy entirely your own, serviceable to your actions and cease imitating the thoughts of others. . . . The other races [h]ave made their heroes, we also can create our own heroes and point our people to them as examples because of their noble deeds. The Universal Negro Improvement Association is seeking to put the Negro in his right position. Whatever the criticisms of the Universal Negro Improvement Association may be, above all that has been said about the Organization, it stands for the loftiest and noblest ideals pertaining to the work of man. There is nothing that the black man has done that the Universal Negro Improvement Association has not inspired him to do through its creed that he should stand on his own.

There is nothing that man cannot do if he applies himself rigorously to do it. We are therefore inspiring you to apply yourselves consistent[l]y, in season and out of se[a]son to what you have decided to do. The Creed of "African Fundamentalism" must be maintained and protected every day. It is a Philosophy that is to serve as a guide to the Negro Peoples of the world. The other peoples do not live their lives by chance, they have a Creed to guide them. Our race is the only one that has not done that, and so long as we continue the slack methods, so long will we be the slaves of the world. God intended that you should rise to every occasion; He gave you the same mental reserve as any other race. He blessed you with the same intelligence as others; but your intelligence has been so warped, so abused as to [m]ake you almost the slave of those who have thought more of life and know how to husband it, so as to get the best out of it.

A Splendid Recommendation

The Universal Negro Improvement Association makes the recommendation and I honestly support this recommendation, that there is such glory and honour for the Negro to attain in the world, as have been achieved and attained by any other race before. There is nothing in nature's law so limited as to prevent the Negro enjoying what the other people are enjoying, which they obtained through method. I tell you, whether it is the thought of Socrates, Plato, or Napoleon; the white race has a system, a method, a code of ethics laid down for the white child to go by, a philosophy, a set Creed to guide its life. When the child comes into the world, this Creed is set out for him to follow and he is trained thereby, so you will not wonder that the white race has reached such a height in civilisation. They will not tell you what is to be found in that Creed, you must find that out for yourselves. We go to the same school that they go to, we study out of the same text books that they study from, yet there are things, many things that the white child knows that you have never seen or heard of. The white child is given private tuition in the knowledge of life. There is no man in the world of one race who will impart to the members of another race the things that would enable that race to launch out successfully in life to compare itself with his race. The Negro must understand that he is *standing by himself.*

If he is to enjoy the best out of life, he must create for himself, and he can only create for himself when he has given to the world his philosophy and code to guide him. And I can recommend to you nothing more enhancing than the Creed we have laid down in "African Fundamentalism." If you will absorb it you will get inspiration to guide you and your children. Take the Jews for example, they have a set philosophy of life; as the Jewish child is born into the world that philosophy is laid before him; he grows in that philosophy, lives and dies in that philosophy. As of the Jews so of the other people. They have set philosophies, that have not been thought out-doors, but within themselves. You, the Negro, bring children into the world without any policy to guide them, when they should have inherited from their fathers a Creed, a policy to advance the race. You will make excuse that you have been in slavery for three hundred years. We excuse you for that; but you have been emancipated now one hundred years, and it is time that you were able to stand upon the same level as the other peoples, understanding nature and nature's laws. When you get to understand that, you will no longer be the cringing creatures as others would have you be; but a master. The opportunity is yours, you can lift your selves any height, as others have done; it is only for you to summon the courage and absorb these things, which are at your doors, and so merit the blessing of God. The Universal Negro Improvement Association is opening the door of intelligence to the Four Hundred Million Negroes of the world—the door of inspiration. Go to the fount and drink, and when you do so you will see all honour in your own race, create your own heroes so that in another generation, I will not have to refer to the heroes of another race, but the teachers will recommend to you the heroes of your own race even though they may have passed this way three thousand years ago. The opportunity is yours to play your part as an Alexander did, as a Constantine did, as a Cortez did, as a C[ae]sar did, as a Napoleon did, as a William the Conqueror did, as the great white men are now playing their part in the world.

Chapter 3

Forbidden Alcohol

Chapter Preface

A s Americans toasted the arrival of the new decade on
New Year's Eve 1920, it would be the last such celebration with legal champagne for more than a decade. On
January 16, 1920, the Eighteenth Amendment to the Constitution became law, ushering in Prohibition and making it
a crime to manufacture, sell, barter, or possess alcoholic
beverages.

Priests, politicians, and other reformers hailed Prohibition, calling it "a noble experiment." Those who opposed alcohol, called "drys," preached that bootleg alcohol under-
mined the willpower, degenerated the character, and made
slaves out of those who drank it. Influential business leaders such as Henry Ford refused to hire anyone who drank so
much as a drop.

Attempts to limit drinking, however honorable their in-
tentions, led to an explosion of lawlessness never before experienced in the United States. Due to political corruption,
wide-open borders, and indifference to the law, Prohibition
was destined to fail from the very beginning.

Any entrepreneur with a few hundred dollars could rent
a storefront or basement, make a deal with a local gangster,
and go into the speakeasy business selling booze to a thirsty
public. While a few dedicated government agents attempted to stem the tide of bootleg liquor washing over America,
many Prohibition agents offered to look the other way after
receiving huge bribes from organized crime. As gangsters
such as Al "Scarface" Capone made millions, the bloody
battles over turf and power made national headlines.

There was one legal way to obtain liquor, however. Physicians were authorized to write prescriptions for alcohol for
medicinal purposes. In an era before modern medicine and
pain-relieving drugs, brandy and whiskey were used by

people during the 1920s to treat everything from a head cold to pain from cancer.

As the United States entered the dark days of the depression in 1929, most desperate, out-of-work Americans could not buy a legal drink. Not until April 7, 1933, was the "noble experiment" put to an end and beer once again gushed forth in saloons and dancehalls across the country.

Selling Bootleg Liquor in New York City

Charlie Berns

Before Prohibition went into effect, bars and saloons were often regulated by city and state ordinances. When alcohol was outlawed in 1920, illegal saloons, called speakeasies, sprang up on nearly every corner. In some areas, entire city blocks were populated with nothing but speakeasies. In New York City, for example, there were about sixteen thousand legal bars prior to Prohibition. After 1920, an estimated one hundred thousand illegal speakeasies opened their doors during the next ten years. Many of these establishments were magnets for prostitution, gambling, and other illegal activities.

In the following excerpt, speakeasy proprietor Charlie Berns explains to freelance author John Kobler how he managed to survive in the rough-and-tumble world of gangsters, corrupt police, and illegal booze.

In 1919, when I was eighteen, I went to the New York University School of Commerce to study accounting. Jack Kriendler was a distant cousin—our families had immigrated from Austria and we lived near each other on the Lower East Side—and he attended Fordham. In the evenings we both worked as salesmen for Jack's uncle, Sam Brenner, who owned a shoe store on the corner of Essex and Rivington streets. He also owned a saloon across the way, and we made ourselves generally useful there as well. For instance, there came a time when the government slapped an additional tax on whiskey of 25 cents a barrel. So whenever the tax collector was due to drop around, Jack and I would cart away a few barrels and hide them at home until the danger passed.

The year I graduated, 1922, Jack and a classmate named Eddie Irving bought a controlling interest in a type of place near the campus known as a "Village [Greenwich Village] tea room." They called it the Redhead. In addition to food they sold liquor in one-ounce flasks, miniatures, which the customers could drink right there if they wished or take home. They asked me to keep the books. They couldn't afford to pay me a salary. So they made me a partner. Our only idea behind the enterprise at the start was to earn enough money to continue our education, I having decided to practice law instead of accountancy and Jack to become a pharmacist. The way things developed, neither of us realized his ambition.

The Redhead served good, solid, simple food—Jack had a natural culinary gift—and the best liquor we could find. We dealt with two neighborhood bootleggers who would deliver the merchandise to Jack's home on East Fourth Street. When we needed fresh supplies, Jack's kid brothers, Mac and Pete, would wheel it over, a few bottles at a time. Who was going to suspect a couple of kids that age? We never did discover the original source of our liquor, but it was always authentic imported stuff.

We attracted a small but choice crowd, young people mostly from the schools and colleges, and an occasional tourist. We were a success. But even before we started, we had been approached by a group of Village gangsters who declared themselves in. Being innocent college boys, we refused to discuss the matter. A couple of weeks later they came around again. They told us unless we paid for certain protective services, they would wreck the joint. We remained unimpressed. A few nights later, as Jack and I were walking home, a couple of them jumped us. We gave a pretty good account of ourselves, and they took quite a licking. The next time I wasn't so lucky. Jack survived in one piece; but my attacker had a razor, and I wound up in St. Vincent's Hospital with a dozen stitches in my throat. A third fight took place a month later, but again we managed to drive them off.

Police Protection

Meanwhile, we had become acquainted with the district police captain through friends in the James Heron Association. This was a very powerful Lower East Side Democratic organization. These friends let the captain know that Jack and Charlie were decent people who ran an orderly place, no bookmaking, no gambling, no hookers. He came to see us. "Why didn't you let me know about these things that have been happening to you?" he asked. Jack said: "We didn't understand how serious it was." "I'll see what we can do," he said. And nobody ever bothered us again the whole time we operated in the Village.

Every speakeasy had to make some arrangements with the cops to survive. In our case it wasn't exactly a shakedown, nothing on a regular basis, more like an act of friendship. We would slip the captain a $50 bill from time to time and a box of cigars to the cops on the beat. They could always count on us for free meals and drinks, and at Christmas time, of course, we had a gift for everybody.

In 1925 we sold the Redhead . . . and opened a place we called the Fronton at 88 Washington Place, a basement nightclub this time with dancing and entertainment. Our star attraction was Al Segal, a great jazz pianist, who later coached performers like Ethel Merman. At the Redhead the door was always open. People just wandered in, paid a 50-cent cover charge on weekend nights and drank their miniature flasks. But the Fronton was a bigger, riskier operation. We felt we had to know our customers. So we kept the front door locked and looked people over carefully through a peephole before we admitted them.

The Fronton prospered, too, and it wasn't long before we heard from our gangster friends again. But we got an unusual break, thanks to a boyhood chum of mine. His name was Jimmy Kerrigan. His father once ran a saloon on Fiftieth Street and Broadway before the Capitol Theater was built there. I peddled newspapers in the area at the age of thirteen, and that's how my path crossed Jimmy's. Well, Jimmy grew up to be a revenue agent, which may explain why we never had any trouble with the feds back at the Redhead.

The minute I got the word from those hoodlums that they were planning to visit us on a certain night I got in touch with Jimmy. He arrived in a car with five of his fellow agents, parked across the street and waited. When the gangsters showed, the agents swarmed all over them. They held a long conversation out there on the sidewalk, and that's the last we ever heard from that particular group.

First a flood, then a flash fire hit the Fronton, and it taught us the importance of having friends in the fire department, as well as the police. Chief Purdy headed the fire brigade nearest us. Off duty he liked to drop in for a few snorts with the missus, and we never charged him anything. One spring day it rained so hard the sewers backed up. Our main room being below street level, the water started rushing up through the toilet bowls and flooding the place. Chief Purdy answered our distress call with powerful pumps and pumped us dry.

Not long after, the flash fire broke out. We never found out how it started. This time Chief Purdy and his men arrived with axes and started to wreck the premises. "Think of all the money you're going to get from the insurance," he said. "My God!" I told him. "We're not insured!" He felt terrible. "Never mind," he said, "we'll fix it all up." And they did, too.

A Friendly Arrest

The construction of the Sixth Avenue subway forced us to abandon the Fronton in 1926, and we moved uptown into a brownstone house with an iron gate at 42 West Forty-ninth Street. The main reason we chose it was that the Italian bootlegger who owned it and wasn't doing too well because he couldn't speak much English agreed to guarantee our mortgage payments if we would buy all our stock from him. We found both him and his liquor reliable. In fact, if we overbought, he would always take back a few cases. We quickly established a reputation for our French and Italian cooking and our cellar.

Soon after we opened, a police captain from the Forty-seventh Street station came to pay his respects and explain that to protect himself, he had to make a friendly arrest—that is, to put it on the record that we sold liquor. "Now you just leave a couple of pints out in the open," he told us. "We'll have a man come by and pick them up. But don't worry. You'll go free on bail, and that'll be the end of the matter." Which is exactly how it worked out.

A certain group of federal agents presented a more serious problem. They were young men of good families, socialites, who saw a means of making some extra easy money by joining the Prohibition Unit. To put it crudely, they were shakedown artists. The way we handled them, a number of us speakeasy operators in the neighborhood created a sort of informal association. John Perona of the Bath Club, who later founded El Morocco, was the main negotiator who spoke for us all. When one of those agents tried to make a case against us, we'd tell him: "You know John Perona. Call him. He'll tell you we're all right and he'll take care of everything." Then we'd square it with John. It cost us about a thousand a year, not including free meals and drinks.

Our Forty-ninth Street place changed its name every year in order to avoid continuity in the IRS records—the Iron Gate, the Gotto, 42, Jack & Charlie's, the Puncheon Club. One evening a Yale student named Ben Quinn came in, took a quick look around and cried: "My God, this is my old home! I grew up here!" He was right. The house had passed through several hands since his father sold it. Ben became a regular visitor, and the place was sometimes called "Ben Quinn's kitchen."

In spite of all the payoffs we did have one serious raid. It was ordered personally by Mabel Walker Willebrandt [the Harding-appointed Assistant Attorney General in charge of prohibition enforcement]. Two things put her on our trail.

Equipping an automobile with a smokescreen device was just one ruse bootleggers used to outwit police.

First, the rumor that we were the only New York speakeasy in continuous operation that had never been bothered by the city police or the feds. Secondly, a valued customer, a Southern gentleman, who didn't trust his local brew, telephoned to ask us to send him some of our whiskey. The employee who took the call stupidly sent it through the mail with the return address on the package. The post office spotted it, reported it to the prohibition authorities and made Mrs. Willebrandt doubly determined to get us, selling liquor through the mail being an additional offense.

It was a long-drawn-out case, but thanks to our able counselor-at-law we reached a compromise. We pleaded guilty to possession of liquor and paid a fine. Ironically, the raid turned out to be the best advertising we ever got. It made us. Because the confiscated liquor was analyzed by federal chemists, who declared it to be of the finest quality. The press cheered. [Journalist] H.L. Mencken wrote, as nearly as I can remember: "Why raid a place that is serving good liquor and not poisoning anybody?"

Although we owned the building on Forty-ninth Street, we only leased the ground, and in 1929 the lease ran out. By then the Rockefellers, who had bought up or leased a lot of land in the Forties and Fifties, including our location, were planning to construct Rockefeller Center. So we had to move again. We didn't want to leave the neighborhood, not after the good relations we had established there with various prohibition agents. We considered several houses in West Fifty-third and West Fifty-fourth, but there were Rockefellers living on both those streets, and they didn't like speakeasies. Nobody exactly liked to have a speakeasy as a neighbor, but some people were more broad-minded than others. We finally settled for the brownstone we've occupied ever since at 21 West Fifty-second.

The last night on Forty-ninth Street, which was not long before a wrecking crew started to tear down the building, we threw a private farewell party for some of our favorite customers. Bea Lillie, for example. And Bob Benchley. We gave every guest a crowbar or spade and let them go to work breaking down the walls and digging up the floor. Then we all loaded the bottles, crockery, furnishings and so forth onto carts and wheeled them three blocks north to our new address.

We weren't there very long before three hoodlums paid us a visit. They represented Jack "Legs" Diamond. [Of all the gang overlords, possibly the most barbarous. The nickname derived from his fleet-footedness as an adolescent thief. It amused him, a kidnapper, as well as bootlegger, hijacker, extortioner and dope dealer, to burn the bare soles of his captives' feet with matches. He killed, or ordered to be killed, dozens of competitors. He himself was shot up so often that the underworld dubbed him "the Clay Pigeon."] It was like the old days in the Village again. Diamond wanted a piece of our business. The doorman threw the hoodlums out. We were lucky. Before Diamond had a chance to strike back at us, he was shot to death.

Not a Drop of Evidence

We continued on friendly terms with the prohibition agents. We also became quite friendly with some of the assistant

U.S. attorneys, who would drop in for an occasional drink or when they needed a good bottle as a gift would ask us to help them out. But you could never be sure. You could never relax completely. Some new officials might be appointed to the New York district or the agents you took care of might be reassigned elsewhere, and the first thing you knew you got raided.

We had this engineer we trusted, and he installed a series of contraptions for us that worked on different mechanical or electrical impulses. For example, the shelves behind the bar rested on tongue blocks. In case of a raid the bartender could press a button that released the blocks, letting the shelves fall backward and dropping the bottles down a chute. As they fell, they hit against angle irons projecting from the sides of the chute and smashed. At the bottom were rocks and a pile of sand through which the liquor seeped, leaving not a drop of evidence. In addition, when the button was pressed, an alarm bell went off, warning everybody to drink up fast. We once put too many bottles on the shelves and they collapsed under the weight. Another time a bartender pressed the button by mistake. But we had only one serious raid. The agents searched the building for twenty-four hours. They never found a single contraption.

The most important was the secret door to our wine cellar. [Here Berns led the author down to the subterranean depths of the building. We paused before an alcove, its white walls bare, and he produced a long, thin steel rod.] Unless you know exactly where to look, all you can see are solid walls, no visible cracks of any kind. But there's this tiny aperture here. You'd have to have an eagle eye. [He shoved the rod through.] When I push this a little further in, you'll hear a noise. That's the tongue lock being released on the other side. It takes very little pressure on my part, even though with the steel frame support the thing weighs over a ton. It works like a trigger on a gun. Listen. [I heard a sharp, metallic click, and the wall swung back on silent hinges, revealing bin upon bin of bottles cradled on their sides.] This is the only entrance or exit. No other way in or out. If the mechanism broke, we'd have to dig through the concrete and pull out the whole lock. But that never happened. And no agent ever discovered the cache either. We still keep the contraption because people like to come down here and see the way things were in the old days.

Memoir of Eliot Ness, Prohibition Agent

Eliot Ness and Oscar Fraley

> The man who most benefited from Prohibition was Al "Scar-face" Capone, a Chicago mobster who was making as much as $100 million a year running distilleries and breweries that supplied booze to speakeasies, bookie joints, gambling houses, and brothels.
>
> Capone's nemesis was Eliot Ness, a special agent of the U.S. Department of Justice and head of the Prohibition bureau in Chicago. Ness assembled a nine-man squad of agents—nicknamed the "Untouchables" because they could not be bribed—to destroy Al Capone and his empire. The agents discovered Capone's breweries, which were disguised as regular warehouses, by following trucks loaded with empty barrels destined to be filled with bootleg liquor. In the excerpt below, Ness describes the method of operation for raiding Scarface's breweries in Chicago.
>
> When Prohibition ended in 1933, Ness served in the U.S. Department of the Treasury and the Federal Security Agency. Between 1959 and 1963, Ness's battles against crime were featured in the television show "The Untouchables."

A way to get inside the breweries came to me as I watched the two captured trucks being driven away [from a place we just raided].

What I needed was a powerful, ten-ton truck with a special steel bumper covering the whole radiator. Then we could

Excerpted from *The Untouchables,* by Eliot Ness with Oscar Fraley (New York: Award Books, 1969). Copyright © 1947 by Eliot Ness and Oscar Fraley.

crash through the steel doors which I assumed must be standard equipment at the Capone breweries.

The next morning I sketched the bumper I had in mind and discussed the idea with [fellow Agent Lyle] Chapman.

"I want that bumper really strong," I told him. "And I'd prefer a flat-bed truck on which we can carry scaling ladders. From now on we're going to be ready for any emergency."

Chapman nodded and suggested several ways to improve on the construction of the oversized bumper.

I turned the project over to him and waited for [Joe] Leeson and [Sam] Seager to report from their cleaning-plant vigil at Thirty-Eighth and Shields. I didn't have long to wait, because that same afternoon, dark circles under his eyes, Leeson came into my office and collapsed into a chair. . . .

The Tail Job

He told me then how they had tailed a load of cleaned barrels from the cleaning plant to a large garage on Cicero Avenue, in Cicero, adjacent to the Western Electric Company. On this move, the barrel truck had a convoy of two gangsters in a souped-up Ford. The hoodlums wore the pearl gray felt hats with the narrow black bands that were the trade-mark of the Capone mobsters.

"There's a field full of tall weeds right across the street from the garage," Leeson related. "Well, we came in from the other side of that vacant lot late yesterday afternoon and kept watch until three o'clock in the morning before anything happened."

At that time, he said, lights went on in the garage, and a truck pulled out with a load of barrels. Apparently word of our [previous] raid had circulated throughout the mob by this time, because the convoy the day before apparently hadn't been aware of anyone tailing it. Obviously this had been going on so long that they had fallen into the habit of paying little attention to their guard duty.

"But when they pulled out of that garage this morning," Leeson explained, "there was a convoy of two Ford coupés loaded with hoods, and they were really on the lookout. Naturally, we had to lay low because those cars scooted around the neighborhood like a couple of rat terriers. From what we could see, this is only a 'cooling off' spot, not a brewery.

"So what do we do now?" he asked after a pause.

"Here's what you do," I told him. "Tonight, find a hiding place near where you saw that truck disappear with the convoy last night and watch its route without being seen. You'll have to follow it step by step, night by night, until you discover where the convoy leaves it and returns to the 'cooling off' garage."

The following night Leeson and Seager resumed their watch and, working on foot, took up from the point at which the barrel truck had disappeared from view. Three days later they were back in my office. Seager's long, hard face bore a grimace.

"How do you like those guys," he growled. "You must have thrown a scare into 'em the other night."

"What's up?" I asked, fearful that they might have been seen.

Leeson laughed at the look on my face, guessing my thoughts.

"Don't worry, they didn't spot us. It's just that after all our work tailing those barrel trucks, they've only been moving them about a block and a half from the garage where they were 'cooled off.'"

The trucks, he said, were being taken on a long, circuitous route to what must be a brewery at 1632 South Cicero Avenue.

"And what do you think?" Leeson grinned. "There's another vacant lot right across the street for our command post." . . .

Rugged-Looking Crew

Within a few days we learned that the only action taking place around the huge warehouse, after the trucks rumbled into its interior in the small hours of the morning, was between four-thirty and five-thirty in the morning.

Crouched in the tall weeds, tin cans and other debris digging into our ribs, knees, and elbows, we saw two ten-ton trucks loaded with empty barrels drive in, while from another direction a tremendous tank truck rumbled in at the same time. After about forty minutes, the barrel trucks reappeared, groaning under their liquid loads, and the obviously lightened tank truck sped away into the darkness. Within a few minutes four or five men, as the case might be, would walk from the darkened building to spots where they had parked their cars in various parts of the neighborhood.

Finally, after several days of watching this procedure, I was convinced that here was the brewery we had been seeking and I began to prepare for a raid.

Meanwhile, I had been filing daily reports with the United States District Attorney's office. . . . It was suggested that I invite the co-operation of Colonel John F.J. Herbert, head of the Chicago prohibition detail, the next time I made a raid.

I called Herbert and told him we were preparing for another raid and that I would like to use one or two of his agents. . . .

Herbert told me that he could spare only one man, a new appointee who had never been on a raid. I jotted down his name and address, and we made arrangements to pick him up at three o'clock the following morning.

I got quite a shock when I drove to his home to get him.

He was a mousy little man with thick, horn-rimmed glasses. I learned later that he had been a clerk in a Chicago department store and had obtained his brand-new job as a prohibition agent through political connections.

He obviously got quite a shock, too, when he stepped into the car with us.

We were a rugged-looking crew, I suppose, to a man unaccustomed to violence. The car's ceiling light polished the high olive cheekbones of [Bill] Gardner, a muscular 240-pounder holding a sawed-off shotgun nonchalantly on his lap. Sitting next to the big Indian was the slate-faced Seager, his 210 pounds always coiled for action. And Chapman's six-foot, one-inch bulk left little room on the front seat between himself and me.

With a meek nod which acknowledged the introductions, the little man slid into the back seat and was almost lost to view between Gardner and Seager.

"Have you got a gun?" I asked him.

"No," he said. "Am I going to need one?"

I fished into the dash pocket and handed a .38 in a shoulder holster back to Seager.

"Show him how to put it on."

Gardner lifted the little man forward with one hand and stripped back his coat with the other. Seager swiftly tied the holster in place and, as if the prohibition man were a doll, they put his coat back on. Once more, he almost disappeared between them.

I had to stifle a chuckle in the darkness as Chapman drove us to a room I had rented on the Chicago East Side. . . .

Planning the Raid

We gathered in the comfortable, old-fashioned front bedroom of a rooming house run by the widow of a one-time Chicago policeman. They'd got no tip-off information from her. Capone's mob had made her a widow.

My whole crew was on hand this time . . . twelve of us. I laid it out for them like a football play, filling them in on the ten-ton flat-bed truck with the special steel bumper which [Frank] Basile had driven to the rendezvous.

"Frank is going to drive that thing right through the front doors of the brewery after our pigeons are safely inside," I said. "I'm going to be riding in the cab with him and the prohibition agent. Chapman is going to ride on the back and drop off just before we crash the doors, covering the hole we've made after we go in. . . .

The raid was planned for 5:00 A.M., the time the barrel trucks should be right in the midst of their loading. Seager's detail, storming the back, was ordered to attack on the dot of five. Meanwhile, [Marty] Lahart and his roof climbers were to meet the truck just a few doors from the brewery at 4:59—leaving them one minute flat to grab their ladders and scale the roof.

"And remember one thing," I cautioned. "Every one of you, whose job is to cover a possible exit, is to hold his position until I personally release you after it's all over."

Not a single prisoner ever had been captured in a raid on a Capone brewery. This time, I thought as I walked down the stairs and out into a crisp, star-filled night, it was going to be different!

South Cicero Avenue, as Basile trundled our truck onto its cobbled surface, was deserted. Nothing moved except our truck and the two cars behind us. The little prohibition man sitting rigidly between Basile and me hadn't spoken a word since we entered the cab. In the glare of a street light I looked at my watch. We were only a block away now; it was 4:58.

Squirming around to look through the back window, I saw Seager's car swing off around the corner and drift out of sight. Sam wouldn't miss, I knew.

Then, a short distance from double doors, Basile coasted to the curb at my signal and Lahart's car halted right behind us. Four figures emerged, and Gardner was a giant shadow against the moon as he swiftly handed down the long extension ladders. . . . The ends of the ladders were muffled, and I knew there would be no grating giveaway as the ladders stretched up against the corner of the brewery and my men swung up out of sight.

"Straight Through the Wall"

The second hand swept up toward the top of my watch. My voice as steady as possible, I directed Basile:

"Hit it, Frank!"

The truck lurched forward with gathering momentum, and Basile had it in second gear when he spun the wheel as the closed doors of the brewery rushed toward us.

I sure hope that bumper does the trick—and that those doors aren't stronger than we are, I was thinking just before we hit with a rending crash.

Splintered wood hurtled down on the radiator, while a flying fragment etched a spider-web design in the windshield glass. My right arm braced against the dashboard, I could feel my left elbow clutched in the terrified grip of the little prohibition man beside me.

Then we were through the doors, as they gave way with a thunderous clap—and my heart sank!

This was no brewery! At least it didn't seem to be, at first glance.

But then I realized that what I was looking at was a wooden wall, painted black, about two truck lengths back from the entrance of the building. It had been designed that

---

The Infamous St. Valentine's Massacre

To the average American, nothing epitomized the lawlessness of Prohibition more than the slaughter of seven gangsters in a Chicago garage on February 14, 1929. Known as the St. Valentine's Day Massacre, the killing was carried out by Al Capone's hit men, who were trying to wipe out a rival gang run by George "Bugs" Moran. As biographer Laurence Bergreen writes, when Capone's killers arrived disguised as policemen, the victims found little reason to resist.

At 10:30 on Thursday morning, the . . . gunmen . . . donned their stolen police uniforms and jumped into a stolen police car. Its gong clanging, the black-and-white pulled up in front of 2122 North Clark Street, and four men rushed out, two wearing overcoats and two police uniforms. They gave every appearance of cops engaged in a routine raid. The four men entered the storefront and walked rapidly through a passageway to the bare, unheated garage at the back, where they came upon seven men. Included were the Gusenberg brothers [Frank and Pete] . . . a safecracker named John May; Albert R. Weinshank, a saloon keeper; James Clark, a bank robber whose real name was Albert Kashellek and who was Moran's brother-in-law; and Adam Heyer, a utility racketeer who served as Moran's "business manager." The seventh member of the group was Dr. Reinhart H. Schwimmer, twenty-nine, a suspiciously prosperous optometrist. Because he alone had no police record, it has generally been assumed that Schwimmer was nothing more than a dapper young doctor who liked to socialize with gangsters for harm-

way to give the illusion of a vacant garage. The brewery had to be behind that false wall. Pointing forward, I barked at Basile:

"Hit it again! Straight on through that wall!"

Frank didn't question me. He threw the truck into low gear, and again there was a grinding crash, only not as loud this time as the black wall collapsed.

---

less amusement. . . . They were a well-dressed, prosperous-looking group of second- and third-tier gangsters, their diamond stickpins and rings glinting in the morning light. Dr. Schwimmer wore a carnation in his lapel. Their security consisted of Heyer's German shepherd, named Highball, who was tied to a pipe. Each man carried several thousand dollars in cash to pay for the shipment of Old Log Cabin [whiskey], and they expected to be joined by Moran and two other associates, Willie Marks and Ted Newberry.

At that moment, ["Machine Gun" Jack] McGurn's "cops" . . . entered the garage. They ordered the seven men gathered there to raise their hands and to line up against the wall. Fooled by the disguise, the men, some of whom carried weapons, obeyed. They offered no struggle, no resistance. After disarming their victims, the four executioners suddenly opened fire on them with two machine guns, a sawed-off shotgun, and a .45. The bullets ripped into the bodies; May and Clark received a blast from the shotgun, and within ten seconds the seven men slumped to the floor of the garage, dead. All except for one man, that is: Frank Gusenberg. Made frantic by the noise and the blood, Heyer's German shepherd sent up a piteous howl heard throughout the neighborhood.

As the four executioners left the scene of the crime, they staged a dumb show designed to confuse witnesses. The men in overcoats placed their hands in the air, while the "cops" followed with their guns trained on them. The four walked deliberately to the stolen police car, got in, and sped away. Witnesses believed they had seen two policemen arresting two suspects, not four assassins escaping the scene of the crime.

Laurence Bergreen, *Capone: The Man and the Era.* New York: Touchstone, 1994.

It went down in a shower of dust and splinters, as if some giant hand had drawn a curtain aside to disclose a tableau. Five men stood there, frozen. As I leaped from the truck before it even stopped rolling, one of them, a huge, grizzled man, started to reach for the gun in his shoulder holster.

My Colt was in my hand, and as he made his move I triggered a shot over his head. His hand dropped away as I shouted over the hollow echo of the shot:

"Hold it! This is a federal raid!"

A man standing at the back inside one of the three trucks ducked, then made a dash toward the rear. Chapman started after him when there was a smacking sound and a groan. Seconds later, Sam Seager appeared out of the shadows, dragging the man by the collar of his coat.

"Guess he didn't hear us coming in the back, you were making so much noise with that truck," Sam grinned. "So I fetched him one to let him know the rest of the Marines had landed."

The man Sam had collared, nursing an eye that was going to have purplish overtones next day, was shoved into line with the other four. They were searched for weapons but only one was armed.

I was jubilant as I looked them over. We had made quite a haul. The armed man was Frank Conta, Scarface's old assistant. The burly, round-shouldered man standing sullenly next to him was Steve Svoboda, Capone's ace brewer. The other three were truck drivers. For some reason, they were short-handed this particular night, but we had netted two big ones, at least. Nobody had escaped.

I climbed a rickety stairway, obviously an escape route to the roof, and called in Lahart and his detail from the top. Back downstairs, I beckoned to the little prohibition man, still standing motionless and white faced beside the truck with which we had crashed through the doors.

"Keep your gun on these birds. And if they move a finger, don't hesitate to let them have it. They're rough and they play for keeps, so you'd better be prepared to do the same thing."

He gulped and moved a few feet closer to the prisoners. Actually, I didn't expect any trouble. They were unarmed and we were all around them as we set about the process of taking inventory and gathering evidence.

One Hundred Barrels a Day

This brewery, I soon saw, was capable of turning out one hundred barrels of beer daily, a production quota which we were to discover later was the general rule in the Capone breweries.

Seven 320-gallon vats lined up in the room, which was cooled automatically so that beer fermented at a slow rate. The brewery was laid out so that each day 320 gallons of wort, or unfermented beer, were brought in by glass-lined tank truck. One hundred barrels would be filled with beer that had been fermented and spiked with carbonated gas.

When our inventory was completed, I had the prisoners taken to the United States Marshal's office. The three trucks, all gleaming new, were sent to the government-contract garage to be held with the two we had already captured. We were starting to gather quite a fleet.

Meanwhile, as we began to destroy the brewing equipment, Chapman noted the numbers of each truck and pump. Later, Chapman's diligent digging uncovered the information that one of the trucks seized on this occasion had been purchased with another truck being used as a trade-in. Circumstances finally connected Al Capone with the purchase and helped tremendously as evidence in the conspiracy case which finally led to his complete undoing.

Quite naturally, I was highly pleased with the results of this night's work. For the first time, a raid on a Capone brewery had netted prisoners, two of them very important ones.

Henry Ford Promotes Prohibition

Henry Ford and Samuel Crowther

> When Henry Ford first offered his workers the astounding sum of five dollars a day to work on his Model T Ford assembly line he shocked the business world with his generosity. But Ford's highly paid assembly line workers were not allowed to drink alcoholic beverages, which were illegal at the time. Ford went so far as to hire detectives to spy on workers at home to make sure they were not drinking. As an influential leader and owner of several newspapers, Ford often sang the praises of Prohibition as he does in the following excerpt taken from his autobiography published immediately after the stock market crash of 1929.

Prohibition is a moral issue. For it is economically right. We now know that anything which is economically right is also morally right. There can be no conflict between good economics and good morals. In fact the one cannot exist without the other. . . .

The system of doing business with high wages and low prices may be called the American system, and since the coming of Prohibition it has welled up so much prosperity that some could not stand it. They made fools of themselves— just as certain kinds of people always do when they come quickly into a degree of wealth.

And thus, although to-day we are just as prosperous as we were last year, we are not quite as prosperous as we were

Excerpted from *Moving Forward,* by Henry Ford with Samuel Crowther (Garden City, NY: Doubleday, 1930).

two years ago. This [depression] has been taken advantage of by those who would destroy the prosperity of the people once and for all to stage a very active campaign to end Prohibition and bring back liquor. Our present industrial system simply cannot work with liquor. The executive who drinks cannot so plan that high wages will result in low prices, while the workman who drinks cannot work intelligently enough to earn high wages. We must choose between drink and poverty on the one hand and Prohibition and prosperity on the other. That is the choice. There is no middle ground. Look at our present situation.

This country has had a temporary set-back in its prosperity. There is no point in dodging that fact. But we have it in our own hands to determine whether we shall continue to slide back or whether we shall stop where we are and go forward again. The people did not move to check their prosperity. The people never move of themselves. They follow their leaders. Many of the men who should have been leading toward a greater and more widely distributed prosperity took their minds off their real work and turned to gambling in the stock market. Many foolish people following these leaders also took to gambling. Those who won and lost large sums of money now find themselves too bewildered to get down to real, solid work. That is to say, the country has been prosperous since booze went out, but for the last two or three years we have had a money drunk. . . .

Total Abstinence

The brain of a man who drinks alcohol cannot be wholly quick and alert. This is not to say that everyone who does not drink alcohol is quick and alert. But in these days a man needs all the brains he can command, and, whatever be the grade of those brains, they will be several grades lower if their owner drinks. I have not drunkards in mind. The drunkard is in the way of being an invalid and needs skilled medical care as greatly as though he were suffering from any other malignant disease. A nation of drunkards would not have to bother about its progress—there would be no progress to bother about. I am concerned with the man who drinks so moderately that he rarely feels its effects and therefore believes that liquor does not harm him—in fact, he becomes indignant at the very suggestion that it might hurt him.

My experience has been that there can be no temporizing whatsoever with liquor. We must have men who can and will use all the brains they possess. Therefore, since the very beginning, we have in our industries enforced the rule of absolute, total abstinence, both in and out of the shops and offices. We have applied this rule without exception, both to executives and to men and in every country in which we operate. We made this rule not merely because we are opposed to the drinking of liquor but because we are opposed to the cultivating of poverty.

The kingdom of poverty is very strongly fortified. It can be conquered only through making industry serve the whole people. We are all very far as yet from achieving this service, but since Prohibition came to this country we have made more rapid strides toward bringing industry around to the real service of humanity than we made during all the previous history of the world. When this service is perfected, we shall have made prosperity universal and have abolished poverty. The nation cannot go forward on this programme—which is the finest of all programmes—unless it has a full complement of brains and initiative. The nearer we approach national total abstinence, the more brains and initiative we shall have at command.

Brains and Booze Do Not Mix

Brains and initiative are dulled by even the occasional use of alcohol. They are made permanently dull by even the most moderate habitual use, and they vanish altogether in the steady, heavy drinker. This is not my opinion out of hand and without regard to the facts. It is founded on the experience of many years of dealing with hundreds of thousands of men comprising all grades of capability from the highest to the lowest. I do not have to inquire whether or not a man is drinking after hours. I can learn everything I need to know just by talking to him about his section of the business. When an executive who has been very keen and capable begins to accept things as they are and to contribute no new, worthwhile ideas whatsoever, I can feel very certain that he is tippling out of hours. I can feel certain because in my experience it has been demonstrated that hardly one per cent of the letdowns in the man who is physically well is due to any cause other than drinking. I have seen a man taking only one or two glasses of wine a day on the advice of his doctor so change mentally as to be useless. Alcohol kills the will power. More than once I have had to remove men whom I greatly liked and respected and who had been very capable just because they decided that a very little liquor out of hours would do them good. I have had to remove them or give them long vacations, not because they were drinking but because they lacked the keenness which their jobs required. Brains and booze will not mix.

Among workmen this condition is not less apparent. Today's manufacturing requires quick, precise work that calls on the brains far more than on the muscles. We have left behind us the time when most men were only so much beef and brawn and were needed only for their strength and endurance. Even in those days the man who did not drink always had more endurance than the man who did, but with nearly everyone drinking, the exceptional man who did not drink never had much of a chance, for his fellows resented his abstinence. In the class of skilled workmen, the differences became more apparent and always the teetotaller was preferred in employment above the drinker of approximately the same ability. I noted that very early in my own working days.

Drinkers Tend to Quit

When I began to manufacture, I surrounded myself with men who did not drink. We had very little money to spend and we could not afford to waste any of it on men who could not be relied on to be always capable of giving their best. We had to watch every penny. As our operations grew and we took on more men, we kept to the same rule just as a matter of course, for a drinking man never seemed to fit. It was not necessary to ask a man whether or not he drank. The man who drank always stood out among his fellows who did not drink—he never did his work so well. If he did not show in his work that he had stopped drinking, then we simply let him go. More often we did not have to enforce the non-drinking rule. It rather enforced itself; the men quickly found out that they could not drink and do their work, so they either stopped drinking or quit. Thus gradually we gathered a force in which the drinkers were very few and all were transients on the way out. It was because we had such a force that back in 1915 we were able to raise our minimum wage to five dollars a day. We could not have paid that wage to a body of drinking men. We could not have paid that wage to a body of sober men if our executives had been drinkers. We were able to pay the wages and prosper exceedingly because everyone concerned was free from the hindrance of liquor.

As the years have passed, the work in our shops has become finer and has called for an increasing amount of skill and intelligence. A man who is working at a machine which is achieving an accuracy of a thousandth of an inch or better needs a keen brain. He needs a fine coordination between hand and brain even if he be only slipping a bolt through a hole. With a trained coordination every job becomes easy—almost effortless. But any use of alcohol at all seems to destroy that exact coordination, and the result is either slow work or spoiled work—or both. And always the work seems hard. The tippler has no great interest in his work. We rarely have to discharge the drinkers. They discharge themselves—a man will not stick at a job on which he is falling down. . . .

The Drinking Man Is a Menace

High-wage industry has to be intelligent from top to bottom and there is absolutely no place in it for the drinking man. If liquor should return—and of course there is no danger of that—then this industrial system we have built up would break down. It could not continue to pay high wages and sell goods cheaply, and for several reasons. First, the efficiency of both management and men would so drop that the high wages would result in dear goods instead of in cheap goods. That would at once restrict the markets. Second, if the people spent a part of their money for drink, then that much purchasing power would be withdrawn from the general market. Third, with the higher prices and lower purchasing power, the volume markets on which industry depends would vanish. Fourth, without these volume markets there could be no really big business and, since only big business can pay the highest wages, we should begin to slump back and be compelled to figure on how little men could be hired to work for instead of, as now, figuring how much we can pay to them.

Under such circumstances I, for one, should not want to continue in business. There would be nothing ahead worth achieving. Working just to get more money is out of the question.

And this is quite aside from the fact that our life today, outside the shops and the offices, is so geared that a drinking man is a menace.

The inevitable consequence of small-scale production is poverty, for if only a small amount of wealth be produced, then there will be only a small pot to divide and everyone's rations will be short. There is no getting away from this. No method can be devised to distribute what is not there to distribute. Prohibition has made it possible for the nation to create a bigger pot of goods than ever before and therefore to have more to distribute and therefore to that extent to drive back the poverty line.

President [Herbert] Hoover has pledged himself to take every step toward the abolishing of poverty. There can be no lessening of poverty unless the Prohibition laws be observed with the most conscientious honesty as anti-poverty laws, the violation of which makes only for human misery. We need that viewpoint. The criminals who wreck banks or peddle narcotics do not create more misery and do not more deeply hurt society in general than the men who bootleg booze. It is wrong, to my mind, to speak of "enforcing" the Prohibition laws as though they were laws imposed by force upon the people and without their consent. These laws were made by the people for their own protection and the people will support the President to any length to which he may find it necessary to go to see that these laws are obeyed and the criminal booze element driven out.

Ours is a highly intelligent people. They are not in the least fooled by the tremendous and well-financed propaganda which hopes to break down Prohibition, destroy prosperity, and reestablish poverty as an institution. The people very well remember just how much the liquor interests in the old days thought of the welfare of the people and also they remember how many politicians these interests then had at their beck and call. A great many are now wondering whether all the old connections have as yet been severed.

Road to Economic Liberty

The number of people who are being honestly deluded concerning the sentiment of this country on the Prohibition question is very small. The anti-Prohibitionists make a great deal of noise but it will be noted that it is always the same people making the same noise. They are really only a stage army marching into the wings and out again. And this a number of politicians will very shortly have brought home to them.

For Prohibition, as the great intelligent rank and file of our people fully realize, marks the opening of the way toward economic liberty. That is the only true liberty; without it no other kind of liberty matters. It would seem that those who would block the road to liberty and attempt to substitute for true liberty the slavery of alcohol would feel upon them the weight of a great responsibility. Those who profess so much concern for the workingman that they would start him drinking again care about as much for him as a dog does about his forty-seventh grand-dad.

This Prohibition question is dynamite. The people established it without the help and against the opposition of the whole race of politicians. We are only now getting an occasional public official who is sincerely and personally in favour of Prohibition. Until the whole political personnel is made over, a difference will seem to exist between the people and their officials. But in the meantime, if any public official wants to discover what dynamite is, let him try to hinder Prohibition.

Chapter 4

Roaring Good Times

Chapter Preface

Nothing symbolized the Jazz Age more than the woman with bobbed hair, dressed in a short skirt and a cloche hat, twirling a long strand of pearls, and drinking a highball.

Liberated from the mindless drudgery of housework by her vacuum cleaner and washing machine, the young flapper could speed down to the local speakeasy in her Model T Ford. There, for a ten-cent cover charge, she could dance the Charleston and Black Bottom to the thrilling rhythms of the African American jazz band that improvised melodies until dawn. The songs glorified drinking, necking, and wearing stockings scandalously rolled down to show the knee.

Cigarette smoking, a habit formerly practiced only by men, was part of this fashion statement. Women even wore oversized pajamas known as "smoking suits" while clutching long cigarette holders in their teeth.

The lucky flapper could meet a new millionaire who had made his fortune in the bootleg whiskey trade or legally through the hyperinflated stock market. Inspired by the pretty and vapid people depicted in F. Scott Fitzgerald's bestseller *The Great Gatsby,* the flapper might dream of attending endless parties in mansions by the sea.

Other flapper reading material included *Whiz Bang* magazine, filled with fashion articles and slang expressions such as "23 Skidoo," "cat's pajamas," and "Oh you kid!"

If she had a creative side, the flapper could sail to Paris to write or paint—or most importantly, drink in the sidewalk café's with the likes of author Ernest Hemingway or painter Pablo Picasso.

While no one knows how many women were real flappers, this image of the quintessential twenties woman was portrayed in hundreds of magazine articles, plays, and movies.

Flappers, Fashion, and a New Morality

Frederick Lewis Allen

> The 1920s were a time of moral upheaval in the United
> States. While parents, politicians, and business leaders wor-
> ried about the communist revolution spreading from Russia to
> the United States, young people were experiencing their own
> form of rebellion that had nothing to do with politics. Jazz
> music, flappers, speakeasies, cigarettes, and so-called "petting
> parties" in Model T Fords frightened American adults almost
> as much as the Red Menace. In the following excerpt, written
> in 1931, Frederick Lewis Allen, editor of the *Atlantic Monthly*
> and *Harper's,* explores the youth revolution of the 1920s.

A first-class revolt against the accepted American order
was certainly taking place during those early years of
the [twenties], but it was one with which [communist
leader] Nikolai Lenin had nothing whatever to do. The
shock troops of the rebellion were not alien agitators, but
the sons and daughters of well-to-do American families,
who knew little about Bolshevism [communism] and cared
distinctly less, and their defiance was expressed not in obscure radical publications or in soap-box speeches, but right
across the family breakfast table into the horrified ears of
conservative fathers and mothers. Men and women were
still shivering at the Red Menace when they awoke to the
no less alarming Problem of the Younger Generation, and
realized that if the Constitution were not in danger, the
moral code of the country certainly was.

This code, as it currently concerned young people, might have been roughly summarized as follows: Women were the guardians of morality; they were made of finer stuff than men and were expected to act accordingly. Young girls must look forward in innocence (tempered perhaps with a modicum of physiological instruction) to a romantic love match which would lead them to the altar and to living-happily-ever-after; and until the "right man" came along they must allow no male to kiss them. It was expected that some men would succumb to the temptations of sex, but only with a special class of outlawed women; girls of respectable families were supposed to have no such temptations. Boys and girls were permitted large freedom to work and play together, with decreasing and well-nigh nominal chaperonage, but only because the code worked so well on the whole that a sort of honor system was supplanting supervision by their elders; it was taken for granted that if they had been well brought up they would never take advantage of this freedom. And although the attitude toward smoking and drinking by girls differed widely in different strata of society and different parts of the country, majority opinion held that it was morally wrong for them to smoke and could hardly imagine them showing the effects of alcohol.

The [First World] War had not long been over when cries of alarm from parents, teachers, and moral preceptors began to rend the air. For the boys and girls just growing out of adolescence were making mincemeat of this code.

Short Skirts, Makeup, and Dancing

The dresses that the girls—and for that matter most of the older women—were wearing seemed alarming enough. In July 1920, a fashion-writer reported in the *New York Times* that "the American woman . . . has lifted her skirts far beyond any modest limitation," which was another way of saying that the hem was now all of nine inches above the ground. It was freely predicted that skirts would come down again in the winter of 1920–21, but instead they climbed a few scandalous inches farther. The flappers wore thin dresses, short-sleeved and occasionally (in the evening) sleeve-less; some of the wilder young things rolled their stockings below their knees, revealing to the shocked eyes of virtue a fleeting glance of shin-bones and knee-cap; and many of them were visibly using cosmetics. "The intoxication of rouge," earnestly explained Dorothy Speare in *Dancers in the Dark,* "is an insidious vintage known to more girls than mere man can ever believe." Useless for frantic parents to insist that no lady did such things; the answer was that the daughters of ladies were doing it, and even retouching their masterpieces in public. Some of them, furthermore, were abandoning their corsets. "The men won't dance with you if you wear a corset," they were quoted as saying.

The Real Fashion Police

The most fashionably clad young ladies of the 1920s wore their skirts above the knee, cut their hair into short "bobs," and offset bare shoulders with dresses featuring plunging necklines. In the first instance of actual "fashion police," preachers and politicians in dozens of states proposed laws that would prohibit women from exposing too much flesh—or even their knees—in public.

The following excerpt from the New York American mag-azine was reprinted by Loren Baritz, professor of history at the State University of New York at Albany.

In Utah a statute providing fine and imprisonment for those who wear on the streets skirts higher than three inches above the ankle is pending. The Philadelphia "moral gown," with its seven and a half inches of "see level," [above the ankle] as one visitor called it, would cease to be moral in Utah if this law goes through.

A bill is before the Virginia legislature which would raise the *décolletage* [low-cut neckline of a dress]—front and back. It provides that no woman shall be permitted to wear a shirt-waist or evening gown displaying more than three inches of her throat. She must not have skirts higher than four inches

The current mode in dancing created still more consternation. Not the romantic violin but the barbaric saxophone now dominated the orchestra, and to its passionate crooning and wailing the fox-trotters moved in what the editor of the Hobart College *Herald* disgustedly called a "syncopated embrace." No longer did even an inch of space separate them; they danced as if glued together, body to body, cheek to cheek. Cried the *Catholic Telegraph* of Cincinnati in righteous indignation, "The music is sensuous, the embracing of partners—the female only half dressed—is absolutely indecent; and the motions—they are such as may not be described, with any respect for propriety, in a family newspaper. Suffice it to say that there are certain houses appropriate

above the ground or any garment of "diaphanous material."

In Ohio a bill has been drafted prescribing that no *décolleté* shall be more than two inches in depth and that no garment composed of any transparent material shall be sold, nor any "garment which unduly displays or accentuates the lines of the female figure."

"And no female over fourteen years of age," says this same measure, "shall wear a skirt which does not reach to that part of the foot known as the instep."

Similar legislation, differing only in the inches above the ground and the inches below the neck, has been offered in New Jersey, South Carolina, Kansas, Iowa, Pennsylvania, and a full dozen other states.

From the three bills actually cited it would seem that, were these to become laws, the dress with its four-inch-high skirt which would be moral in Virginia would be immodest in Utah, while both the Utah and Virginia skirts would be wicked enough in Ohio to make their wearers subject to fine or imprisonment. Undoubtedly, other state laws would add to this confusion, and therefore a standardization acceptable to all is something that might ultimately be welcomed by women.

Loren Baritz, *The Culture of the Twenties.* Indianapolis: Bobbs-Merrill, 1970.

for such dances; but those houses [of prostitution] have been closed by law."

Drinking and "Petting"

Supposedly "nice" girls were smoking cigarettes—openly and defiantly, if often rather awkwardly and self-consciously. They were drinking—somewhat less openly but often all too efficaciously. There were stories of daughters of the most exemplary parents getting drunk—"blotto," as their companions cheerfully put it—on the contents of the hip-flasks of the new prohibition régime, and going out joyriding with men at four in the morning. And worst of all, even at well-regulated dances they were said to retire where the eye of the most sharp-sighted chaperon could not follow, and in darkened rooms or in parked cars to engage in the unspeakable practice of petting and necking.

It was not until F. Scott Fitzgerald, who had hardly graduated from Princeton and ought to know what his generation was doing, brought out *This Side of Paradise* in April 1920, that fathers and mothers realized fully what was afoot and how long it had been going on. Apparently the "petting party" had been current as early as 1916, and was now widely established as an indoor sport. "None of the Victorian mothers—and most of the mothers were Victorian—had any idea how casually their daughters were accustomed to be kissed," wrote Mr. Fitzgerald. ". . . Amory saw girls doing things that even in his memory would have been impossible: eating three-o'clock, after-dance suppers in impossible cafés, talking of every side of life with an air half of earnestness, half of mockery, yet with a furtive excitement that Amory considered stood for a real moral let-down. But he never realized how widespread it was until he saw the cities between New York and Chicago as one vast juvenile intrigue." The book caused a shudder to run down the national spine; did not Mr. Fitzgerald represent one of his well-nurtured heroines as brazenly confessing, "I've kissed dozens of men. I suppose I'll kiss dozens more"; and another heroine as saying to a young man *(to a young man!),* "Oh, just one person in fifty has any glimmer of what sex is. I'm hipped on Freud and all that, but it's rotten that every bit of real love in the world is ninety-nine per cent passion and one little *soupçon* of jealousy"?

It was incredible. It was abominable. What did it all mean? Was every decent standard being thrown over? Mothers read the scarlet words and wondered if they themselves "had any idea how often their daughters were accustomed to be kissed." . . . But no, this must be an exaggerated account of the misconduct of some especially depraved group. Nice girls couldn't behave like that and talk openly about passion. But in due course other books appeared to substantiate the findings of Mr. Fitzgerald: *Dancers in the Dark, The Plastic Age, Flaming Youth.* Magazine articles and newspapers reiterated the scandal. To be sure, there were plenty of communities where nice girls did not, in actual fact, "behave like that"; and even in the more sophisticated urban centers there were plenty of girls who did not. Nevertheless, there was enough fire beneath the smoke of these sensational revelations to make the Problem of the Younger Generation a topic of anxious discussion from coast to coast.

Moral Backlash

The forces of morality rallied to the attack. Dr. Francis E. Clark, the founder and president of the Christian Endeavor Society, declared that the modern "indecent dance" was "an offense against womanly purity, the very fountainhead of our family and civil life." The new style of dancing was denounced in religious journals as "impure, polluting, corrupting, debasing, destroying spirituality, increasing carnality," and the mothers and sisters and church members of the land were called upon to admonish and instruct and raise the spiritual tone of these dreadful young people. President Murphree of the University of Florida cried out with true Southern warmth, "The low-cut gowns, the rolled hose and short skirts are born of the Devil and his angels, and are carrying the present and future generations to chaos and destruction." A group of Episcopal churchwomen in New York, speaking with the authority of wealth and social position (for they included [millionaire's wives such as] Mrs. J. Pierpont Morgan, Mrs. Borden Harriman, Mrs. Henry Phipps, Mrs. James Roosevelt, and Mrs. E.H. Harriman), proposed an organization to discourage fashions involving an "excess of nudity" and "improper ways of dancing." The Y.W.C.A. conducted a national campaign against immodest dress among high-school girls, supplying newspapers with printed matter carrying headlines such as "Working Girls Responsive to Modesty Appeal" and "High Heels Losing Ground Even in France." . . .

Meanwhile innumerable families were torn with dissension over cigarettes and gin and all-night automobile rides. Fathers and mothers lay awake asking themselves whether their children were not utterly lost; sons and daughters evaded questions, lied miserably and unhappily, or flared up to reply rudely that at least they were not dirty-minded hypocrites, that they saw no harm in what they were doing and proposed to go right on doing it. From those liberal clergymen and teachers who prided themselves on keeping step with all that was new, came a chorus of reassurance: these young people were at least franker and more honest than their elders had been, having experimented for themselves would they not soon find out which standards were outworn and which represented the accumulated moral wisdom of the race? Hearing such hopeful words many good people took heart again. Perhaps this flare-up of youthful passion was a flash in the pan, after all. Perhaps in another year or two the boys and girls would come to their senses and everything would be all right again.

They were wrong, however. For the revolt of the younger generation was only the beginning of a revolution in manners and morals that was already beginning to affect men and women of every age in every part of the country.

Reasons for the Revolution

A number of forces were working together and interacting upon one another to make this revolution inevitable.

First of all was the state of mind brought about by the war and its conclusion. A whole generation had been infected by the eat-drink-and-be-merry-for-tomorrow-we-die spirit which accompanied the departure of the soldiers to the training camps and the fighting front. There had been an epidemic not only of abrupt war marriages, but of less conventional liaisons. In France, two million men had found themselves very close to filth and annihilation and very far from the American moral code and its defenders; prostitution had followed the flag and willing mademoiselles from Armentières had been plentiful; American girls sent over as nurses and war workers had come under the influence of continental manners and standards without being subject to the rigid protections thrown about their continental sisters of the respectable classes; and there had been a very widespread and very natural breakdown of traditional restraints, reticences and taboos. It was impossible for this generation to return unchanged when the ordeal was over. Some of them had acquired under the pressure of war-time conditions a new code which seemed to them quite defensible; millions of them had been provided with an emotional stimulant from which it was not easy to taper off. Their torn nerves craved the anodynes of speed, excitement, and passion. They found themselves expected to settle down into the humdrum routine of American life as if nothing had happened, to accept the moral dicta of elders who seemed to them still to be living in a Pollyanna land of rosy ideals which the war had killed for them. They couldn't do it, and they very disrespectfully said so.

"The older generation had certainly pretty well ruined this world before passing it on to us," wrote one of them (John F. Carter in the *Atlantic Monthly,* September 1920), expressing accurately the sentiments of innumerable contemporaries. "They give us this thing, knocked to pieces, leaky, red-hot, threatening to blow up; and then they are surprised that we don't accept it with the same attitude of pretty, decorous enthusiasm with which they received it, way back in the 'eighties.". . .

The revolution was accelerated also by the growing independence of the American woman. She won the suffrage in 1920. She seemed, it is true, to be very little interested in it once she had it; she voted, but mostly as the unregenerate men about her did, despite the efforts of women's clubs and the League of Women Voters to awaken her to womanhood's civic opportunity; feminine candidates for office were few, and some of them—such as Governor Ma Ferguson of Texas—scarcely seemed to represent the starry-eyed spiritual influence which, it had been promised, would presently ennoble public life. Few of the younger women could rouse themselves to even a passing interest in politics: to them it was a sordid and futile business, without flavor and without hope. Nevertheless, the winning of the suffrage had its effect. It consolidated woman's position as man's equal.

Freed from Household Drudgery

Even more marked was the effect of woman's growing independence of the drudgeries of housekeeping. Smaller houses were being built, and they were easier to look after. Families were moving into apartments, and these made even less claim upon the housekeeper's time and energy. Women were learning how to make lighter work of the preparation of meals. Sales of canned foods were growing, the number of delicatessen stores had increased three times as fast as the population during the decade 1910–20, the output of bakeries increased by 60 per cent during the decade 1914–24. Much of what had once been housework was now either moving out of the home entirely or being simplified by machinery. The use of commercial laundries, for instance, increased by 57 per cent between 1914 and 1924. Electric washing-machines and electric irons were coming to the aid of those who still did their washing at home; the manager of the local electric power company at "Middletown," a typical small American city, estimated in 1924 that nearly 90 per cent of the homes in the city already had electric irons. The housewife was learning to telephone her shopping orders, to get her clothes ready-made and spare herself the rigors of dress-making, to buy a vacuum cleaner and emulate the lovely carefree girls in the magazine advertisements who banished dust with such delicate fingers. Women were slowly becoming emancipated from routine to "live their own lives."

And what were these "own lives" of theirs to be like? Well, for one thing, they could take jobs. Up to this time girls of the middle classes who had wanted to "do something" had been largely restricted to school-teaching, social-service work, nursing, stenography, and clerical work in business houses. But now they poured out of the schools and

Prohibition, coupled with the younger generation's more rebellious attitude, led to a new moral standard during the 1920s. Here, a flapper reveals her secret hiding place for illegal liquor—an ankle flask.

colleges into all manner of new occupations. They besieged the offices of publishers and advertisers; they went into tea-room management until there threatened to be more pur-veyors than consumers of chicken patties and cinnamon toast; they sold antiques, sold real estate, opened smart lit-tle shops, and finally invaded the department stores. In 1920 the department store was in the mind of the average college girl a rather bourgeois institution which employed "poor shop girls"; by the end of the decade college girls were standing in line for openings in the misses' sportswear de-partment and even selling behind the counter in the hope that some day fortune might smile upon them and make them buyers or stylists. Small-town girls who once would have been contented to stay in Sauk Center all their days were now borrowing from father to go to New York or Chicago to seek their fortunes—in Best's or Macy's or Mar-shall Field's. Married women who were encumbered with children and could not seek jobs consoled themselves with the thought that home-making and child-rearing were really "professions," after all. No topic was so furiously discussed at luncheon tables from one end of the country to the other as the question of whether the married woman should take a job, and whether the mother had a right to. And as for the unmarried woman, she no longer had to explain why she worked in a shop or an office; it was idleness nowadays, that had to be defended.

With the job—or at least the sense that the job was a pos-sibility—came a feeling of comparative economic indepen-dence. With the feeling of economic independence came a slackening of husbandly and parental authority. Maiden aunts and unmarried daughters were leaving the shelter of the family roof to install themselves in kitchenette apart-ments of their own. For city-dwellers the home was steadi-ly becoming less of a shrine, more of a dormitory—a place of casual shelter where one stopped overnight on the way from the restaurant and the movie theater to the office. Yet even the job did not provide the American woman with that complete satisfaction which the management of a mechanized home no longer furnished. She still had energies and emotions to burn; she was ready for the revolution. . . .

Effect of Prohibition

When the Eighteenth Amendment was ratified, prohibition seemed, . . . to have an almost united country behind it. Evasion of the law began immediately, however, and strenuous and sincere opposition to it—especially in the large cities of the North and East—quickly gathered force. The results were the bootlegger, the speakeasy, and a spirit of deliberate revolt which in many communities made drinking "the thing to do." From these facts in turn flowed further results: the increased popularity of distilled as against fermented liquors, the use of the hip-flask, the cocktail party, and the general transformation of drinking from a masculine prerogative to one shared by both sexes together. The old-time saloon had been overwhelmingly masculine; the speakeasy usually catered to both men and women. As Elmer Davis put it, "The old days when father spent his evenings at Cassidy's bar with the rest of the boys are gone, and probably gone forever; Cassidy may still be in business at the old stand and father may still go down there of evenings, but since prohibition mother goes down with him." Under the new regime not only the drinks were mixed, but the company as well.

Meanwhile a new sort of freedom was being made possible by the enormous increase in the use of the automobile, and particularly of the closed car. (In 1919 hardly more than 10 per cent of the cars produced in the United States were closed; by 1924 the percentage had jumped to 43, by 1927 it had reached 82.8.) The automobile offered an almost universally available means of escaping temporarily from the supervision of parents and chaperons, or from the influence of neighborhood opinion. Boys and girls now thought nothing, as the Lynds pointed out in *Middletown,* of jumping into a car and driving off at a moment's notice—without asking anybody's permission—to a dance in another town twenty miles away, where they were strangers and enjoyed a freedom impossible among their neighbors. The closed car, moreover, was in effect a room protected from the weather which could be occupied at any time of the day or night and could be moved at will into a darkened byway or a country lane. The Lynds quoted the judge of the juvenile court in "Middletown" as declaring that the automobile had become a "house of prostitution on wheels," and cited the fact that of thirty girls brought before his court in a year on charges of sex crimes, for whom the place where the offense had occurred was recorded, nineteen were listed as having committed it in an automobile.

A Chance Encounter with a Flapper

Ben Hecht

Ben Hecht is the author of novels and short stories inspired by the colorful characters he met while working as a reporter for the Chicago *Journal* and Chicago *Daily News* during the Jazz Age. In the following autobiographical excerpt, Hecht describes a chance encounter with a flapper, her fashion sense, and her trendy slang.

The newspaper man put on his last year's straw hat and went into the street, taking his pensiveness with him. Warm. Rows of arc lights. A shifting crowd. There are some streets that draw aimless feet. The blazing store fronts, clothes shops, candy shops, drugstores, Victrola shops, movie theatres invite with the promise of a saturnalia [wild celebration] in suspense.

At Wilson Avenue and Sheridan Road the newspaper man paused. Here the loneliness he had felt in his bedroom seemed to grow more acute. Not only his own aimlessness, but the aimlessness of the staring, smiling crowd afflicted him.

Then out of the babble of faces he heard his name called. A rouged young flapper, high heeled, short skirted and a jaunty green hat. One of the impudent little swaggering boulevard promenaders who talk like simpletons and dance like Salomes, who laugh like parrots and ogle like Pierrettes [clowns]. The birdlike strut of her silkened legs, the brazen lure of her stenciled child face, the lithe grimace of her adolescent body under the stiff coloring of her clothes were a part of the blur in the newspaper man's mind.

She was one of the things he fumbled for on the typewriter—one of the city products born of the tinpan bacchanal of the cabarets. . . . The caricature of savagery that danced to the caricature of music from the jazz bands. The newspaper man smiled. Looking at her he understood her. But she would not fit into the typewritten phrases.

"Wilson Avenue," he thought, as he walked beside her chatter. "The wise, brazen little virgins who shimmy and toddle, but never pay the fiddler. She's it. Selling her ankles for a glass of pop and her eyes for a fox trot. Unhuman little piece. A cross between a macaw and a marionette."

"I Say 'Razzberry'"

Thus, the newspaper man thinking and the flapper flapping, they came together to a cabaret in the neighborhood. The orchestra filled the place with confetti of sound. Laughter, shouts, a leap of voices, blazing lights, perspiring waiters, faces and hats thrusting vivid stencils through the uncoiling tinsel of tobacco smoke.

On the dance floor bodies hugging, toddling, shimmying; faces fastened together; eyes glassy with incongruous ecstasies.

The newspaper man ordered two drinks of moonshine and let the scene blur before him like a colored picture puzzle out of focus. Above the music he heard the childishly strident voice of the flapper:

"Where you been hiding yourself? I thought you and I were cookies. Well, that's the way with you Johns. But there's enough to go around, you can bet. Say boy! I met the classiest John the other evening in front of the Hopper. Did he have class, boy! You know there are some of these fancy Johns who look like they were the class. But are they? Ask me. Nix. And don't I give them the berries, quick? Say, I don't let any John get moldy on me. Soon as I see they're heading for a dumb time I say 'razzberry.' And off your little sugar toddles."

"How old are you?" inquired the newspaper man abstractedly.

"Eighteen, nosey. Why the insult? I got a new job yesterday with the telephone company. That makes my sixth job this year. Tell me that ain't going good? One of the Johns I met in front of the Edgewater steered me to it. He turned out kind of moldy, and say! he was dumb. But I played along and got the job.

"Say, I bet you never noticed my swell kicks." The flapper thrust forth her legs and twirled her feet. "Classy, eh? They go with the lid pretty nice. Say, you're kind of dumb yourself. You've got moldy since I saw you last."

"How'd you remember my name?" inquired the newspaper man.

"Oh, there are some Johns who tip over the oil can right from the start. And you never forget them. Nobody could forget you, handsome. Never no more, never. What do you say to another shot of hootch? The stuff's getting rottener and rottener, don't you think? Come on, swallow. Here's how. Oh, ain't we got fun!"

A Symbol of New Sin

The orchestra paused. It resumed. The crowd thickened. Shouts, laughter, swaying bodies. A tinkle of glassware, snort of trombones, whang of banjos. The newspaper man looked on and listened through a film.

The brazen patter of his young friend rippled on. A growing gamin [streetwise] coarseness in her talk with a nervous, restless twitter underneath. Her dark child eyes, perverse under their touch of black paint, swung eagerly through the crowd. Her talk of Johns, of dumb times and moldy times, of classy times and classy memories varied only slightly. She liked dancing and amusement parks. Automobile riding not so good. And besides you had to be careful. There were some Johns who thought it cute to play caveman. Yes, she'd had a lot of close times, but they wouldn't get her. Never, no, never no more. Anyway, not while there was music and dancing and a whoop-de-da-da in the amusement parks.

The newspaper man, listening, thought, "An infant gone mad with her dolls. Or no, vice has lost its humanness. She's the symbol of new sin—the unhuman, passionless whirligig of baby girls and baby boys through the cabarets."

They came back from a dance and continued to sit. The din was still mounting. Entertainers fighting against the racket. Music fighting against the racket. Bored men and women finally achieving a bedlam and forgetting themselves in the artifice of confusion.

The newspaper man looking at his young friend saw her taking it in. There was something he had been trying to fathom about her during her breathless chattering. She talked, danced, whirled, laughed, let loose giggling cries. And yet her eyes, the part that the rouge pot or the bead stick couldn't reach, seemed to grow deader and deader.

The jazz band let out the crash of a new melody. The voices of the crowd rose in an "ah-ah-ah." Waiters were shoving fresh tables into the place, squeezing fresh arrivals around them.

The flapper had paused in her breathless rigmarole of Johns and memories. Leaning forward suddenly she cried into the newspaper man's ear above the racket:

"Say this is a dumb place."

The newspaper man smiled.

"Ain't it, though?" she went on. There was a pause and then the breathless voice sighed. She spoke.

"Gee!"—with a laugh that still seemed breathless—"gee, but it's lonely here!"

The Jumpin', Jivin' Jazz Life

Cab Calloway and Bryant Rollins

Dressed in his trademark white zoot suit, Cab Calloway was one of the kings of swing during the Jazz Age, singing, dancing, and leading bands in the hottest clubs of Chicago, New York, and Hollywood. His 1931 song "Minnie the Moocher" made him famous as the scat-singing "hi-de-ho" man who appeared in many movies including 1980's *The Blues Brothers*. In the excerpt below, Calloway talks about life as an African American musician touring the segregated United States in the twenties and the fabled jazz musicians he met on the road.

I'll never forget the way that I left Baltimore. . . . I pawned [my drums] to buy a suitcase to carry my one suit, three shirts, and a suit of underwear. It cost $10, and I gave all the rest of my money to Mama. The show was only paying around $30 and I was used to making more than that. I was still sending it all back to Mama. Those were lean times, but I dug the show and being on the road so much that it didn't matter.

It was my first time on the road as a professional, and I went as wild as a March hare. I chased all the broads in the show and caught one finally, a Japanese-looking colored gal, light-skinned and big and fine. I went for her and she went for me, and we made it together the whole trip. We traveled for about eight weeks, from Baltimore, to Pittsburgh, then

Detroit, and on to Columbus, Ohio. In those days we used to call it the T.O.B.A. Circuit. It stood for Theatrical Organization and Benevolent Association, but it was the circuit all the Negro bands and shows followed and we used to call T.O.B.A. (Tough on Black Asses). We moved from town to town by bus across those bumpy roads and usually in the dead of the night, sleepy as hell after a show in one town, rushing to get into the next town in time to rehearse the new band and open the following night. Negroes weren't allowed to stay in any of the main hotels in the places we played, so everywhere we went the company had a list of Negro families that would rent us rooms. The twenty-five of us would be spread out all around town, and these beautiful folks would rent a room and feed us some of the best damned cooking around for $10 a week. They'd always say it was a pleasure, even an honor, for them to be housing members of such a famous company. They were mainly middle-class, working, churchgoing people who had small, wood-frame, two-story houses with comfortable sofas in the living room and lace curtains. I've always appreciated the kind of treatment black people gave Negro musicians and entertainers who were on the road. Thousands of people in the Midwest and South opened their homes to hundreds of musicians, singers, dancers, and comedians. We couldn't have done those road shows if it hadn't been for such people, warm, loving, gentle folk who treated us like family for the week or two we were in their town. That practice existed until the forties, when some of the lily-white hotels began to admit Negro entertainers. . . .

Chicago: What a City!

After Pittsburgh, Detroit, and Columbus, we hit Chicago. What a city! What a world I had been missing. There were so many people and so many buildings, and so many things to do. And the music. Chicago was just full of music.

In those days the South Side in Chicago was to jazz what Harlem [in New York City] came to be a few years later. There were basically two groups of musicians there, the

white and the colored, and I was fascinated by both. Two of
the best white ones were Eddie Condon and Red McKenzie.
By the time I got to Chicago, they had combined bands into
the McKenzie-Condon Chicagoans. Bix Beiderbecke and
Pee Wee Russell were around Chicago then, and Bud Free-
man, Mezz Mezzrow, Muggsy Spanier, Benny Goodman,
Art Hodes, Harvey Brown, Wild Bill Davidson, Rosey
McHargue—and I think Gene Krupa might have been out
there then too. The colored bands were led, of course, by
Louis Armstrong. King Oliver and his band had just left
Chicago when I got there, so I had to wait until I got to New
York to hear his music, and by then he was on the way
down. Jimmy Noone was over at a club called The Nest
with his group. In 1929 Earl Hines moved his new band into
the Grand Terrace, a beautiful new club on the South Side
and one of the few places in the city where both black and
white patrons were served.

I moved in with [my sister] Blanche at first. She had an
apartment on South Parkway on the South Side. She was
making it pretty well and we had six or seven rooms.
Blanche was living with a guy named Watty. I never even
knew his last name. I just called him Watty. Watty was a
hustler. He played the horses and gambled and seemed to
make a hell of a lot of money. He ran games, too—crap
games and card games—all around Chicago. And from time
to time he'd go out to Fort Wayne or Gary, Indiana, places
like that, and stay for four or five days gambling and running games. He was always hustling and he always had a lot
of money. Later on he wound up with a stable of horses. I
never did know how many he had. He raced them on tracks
in the Midwest. Watty was quite a character. A solid dress-
er, very sharp all the time, and slick to talk to. He could talk
a cat into buying air. He had a beautiful car, a 1925 Lincoln.
He and the other hustlers would park these big old cars on
Thirty-fifth Street in front of the barbershop and spend the
afternoon shooting craps or just talking. Then they'd go out
in the evenings to the gambling rooms around town and
drink and gamble.

I admired Watty because he was living exactly the kind of life he wanted to and was successful at it. But I never got into that life. Watty always saw me as a kid and maybe something of a square from Baltimore, although in those days, in my own eyes, I was just as sophisticated as I could be. Anyhow, he took a liking to me, and eventually helped me to get some gigs. He knew just about all the club owners on the South Side.

College and Singing

We had arrived in Chicago at the end of the summer. [A theatrical production of] *Plantation Days* played at the Grand Theatre on State Street for a couple of weeks, and the crowds were incredible. I had never seen crowds like that before. The people jumped up and down in the theater and had a hell of a time. Then, after two weeks, the show closed, and Blanche took me down to Crane College and helped me enroll. I started classes right away. The studying was pretty heavy, and I was determined to make it in college so for a while I buried myself in my books and forgot everything else. But after about four months, around January of 1928 when I had just turned twenty, I asked Blanche and Watty if they knew somewhere that I could do some part-time singing. I was sure I could handle both studying and singing. Watty took me to a place called the Dreamland Cafe down on State Street. That was my first nightclub gig in Chicago. It was a corny club, but it was crowded every night. The people came in to drink and talk, not to listen to the music, and it was always noisy. It was also small and a little shabby, but I didn't care. I was singing in Chicago. I was making it. They had a little trio in there, and we would do popular tunes and jazz. It was nothing special, but it was special to me.

I began to make some friends around that time, too. Blanche and Watty belonged to a pretty fast group of show people and hustlers, and I was the student who had to be up every morning to get to school, but I had a cousin, William Credit, who was in Crane College and who I had known in

Dowingtown. Through him I met a number of students who lived in Chicago. We used to hang out together, and have a ball partying on the weekends. . . .

It was a different kind of life when I started to sing again. I didn't really have the time to study, so I started to cheat a bit. I had a little girl who used to do my work. She would write my papers and help me to get ready for tests. Thelma Eubanks was her name. I needed her help because I was beginning to get into everything again, just like I had in high school. I was playing basketball with the Crane team, lousy as it was, going to classes days, and singing nights and on weekends. On a typical day, I usually had to make class around ten. No breakfast, just get up and go. Blanche and Watty were night people, and the house was dead when I got up. After I got to know Watty he let me take his car to school. I'd finish classes around three or so and bring the car back and then go out and hang out on the corner with the kids or go on to basketball. I'd be home around five in the evening and have dinner with Blanche—Blanche was a damned good cook—and then I'd go on and make the gig.

A Real Swinger

We had shows every night. They'd start at 8:30 or 9:00 and the last show would be around midnight. I'd get home at 3:30 or 4:00 in the morning, sleep a few hours, and then off to school again. Some days, of course, I didn't make it to class, though God knows I tried. Weekends were tougher than weekdays. We had three shows on Saturdays and Sundays at the Dreamland Cafe. They worked my ass off and paid me as little as they could. I guess I made around $50 a week, and sent most of it home to Mama. That didn't leave me much to live on, and I didn't like the idea of Blanche and Watty carrying my load, so I pitched in with them to help keep up the apartment. As soon as I could, I wanted to get my own place. I couldn't wait to be on my own.

After a few months in the Dreamland, Watty told me he could get me into the Sunset Cafe. Now, that was class. The Sunset was the most popular club on the South Side, farther down on the Thirty-fifth Street strip where most of the good jazz was being played in those days. Right across the street was the Plantation Club, and next to that was The Nest. The Sunset was a real swinger, like the Cotton Club in New York, with beautiful chorus girls, a ten-piece band, comedians, and solo tap dancers. Carroll Dickerson had the band in there at first, and then Louis Armstrong joined Dickerson. I was the house singer. That was the first time I met Louis, although I had admired him for years. His singing and playing have always got to me. I could never understand how a man had so many talents. And in addition, he was a person you could talk to. We became friendly the six months we were together in the Sunset. Two years later, Louis got me my first real big job in New York City. Louis was not as well known around Chicago at that time as guys like Dickerson, the violinist who led his own band and later helped to put together Louis' famous New York City band. That band was breaking it up at Connie's Inn in Harlem in 1929 when I finally got to New York City.

Most of the colored bands around Chicago at that time were playing what they called "Chicago jazz," a mixture of dixieland and swing, with a lot of solos thrown in. Louis's favorite songs at that time were things like "Muskrat Ramble," "Gut-Bucket Blues," "You're Next," and "Oriental Strut." All of the songs he did were full of fire and rhythm, and he was scat singing even then. I suppose that Louis was one of the main influences in my career. Later on I began to scat sing in the Cotton Club with all of that hi-de-hoing. Louis first got me freed up from straight lyrics to try scatting.

Besides Louis there were some other great entertainers and musicians at the Sunset on and off. Mae Alix was probably the best dancer. She had an act where she would tap and ballet and sing for half an hour. At the end of her act, she would dash across the stage and slide into a full split, skidding right up to a ringside table, and the guy would put some money down her dress, and she'd do it again and again, until she had about $20 or $25 per show. She was cleaning up.

It was a treat working with such talent. After a few weeks in the Sunset, I stopped playing drums and just sang. I was doing one of the leading numbers with the great Adelaide Hall. She was a year older than me and could sing her tail off. Later on, in New York, she starred in the Cotton Club's fabulous *Blackbirds* revues of the late twenties and early thirties. Then she joined Duke Ellington's band and went with him to England in 1935. She loved London so much that she settled there, singing in the music halls, and eventually established a nightclub of her own. Adelaide had one of these funky low voices and she used to just growl into the mike sometimes, sexy and bluesy as all get out. She and Ada Brown were the two female leads in the show; the male leads were Jazz Lips Richardson, who got top billing, and Walter Richardson. From time to time, there was also a great team in the show named Brown and McGraw. They were from the old tap-dancing, soft-shoe tradition.

The Sunset Cafe was a fairly large room; it could seat around 250 people and had a large dance floor in the middle. There were murals of dancers and jazz players on the walls and the lights were always down low.

The Money Was Good

As soon as Watty got me this gig in the Sunset Cafe, things began to happen. For one thing my salary shot up to $65 a week, and within a year I was on the way. Things developed so fast that by the spring of 1929 I was married, I had lots of real money for the first time, and I was leading my own band, The Alabamians, as the house band at the Sunset. What had seemed like a dream when I left Baltimore with *Plantation Days* had suddenly become a reality. I was only twenty-one years old, and I was making it. A combination of talent and good luck put me there.

I got a big break about two months after I went into the Sunset Cafe as part of the revue. Right away I became friendly with Ralph Cooper of the dance team of Rector and Cooper. Ralph was also the master of ceremonies for the show. He was doing a hell of a good job, but he was sometimes a little unreliable. Ralph would just take off for a couple of days and nobody would know where the hell he was. One week, when he missed a few shows, the club's owner, Joe Glaser, asked me to take over as M.C. I jumped at the chance, and Glaser thought I was something else. When my buddy Ralph Cooper came back, he was out of a job. We remained friends, and to this day Ralph and I joke over that. Ralph went on to New York eventually, and became a star in Negro theater of the thirties and forties. He played in most of the great Negro musicals and shows before and after World War II, but at that point, he was out of a job. So there I was, in the spring of 1928, suddenly the master of ceremonies at one of the nicest clubs on the South Side. I stayed in the Sunset Cafe, with that revue, through the rest of 1928. The money was pretty good and I was having a good time. I was also still at Crane College, but just barely. . . .

A Band of My Own

Around the spring of 1929, Marion Hardy brought his band, The Alabamians, into the Sunset Cafe. The Alabamians were a fine, hot, jazzy 11-piece band of Chicago boys. Hardy's group replaced Louis Armstrong when Louis and Carroll Dickerson and their band left Chicago for Connie's Inn in Harlem. Louis and Dickerson had been breaking things up at the Sunset and all over Chicago for several years. Their band had included, at various times, Earl "Father" Hines, Jimmy Noone, Erskine Tate, clarinetist Johnny Dodds and drummer Baby Dodds, trombonist Kid Ory, Louis's wife, Lil Hardin, and a bunch of other great musicians.

When the Alabamians came into the Sunset they were being led by Lawrence Harrison. . . . Young Harrison led the group and played violin, but he didn't have the drive to really develop the band, or the looseness to make music sound the way it should. They were playing both pop and jazz and some novelty numbers where the leader would sing a lyric and the band would respond, but Harrison just didn't have the fire that the band needed to reach its potential.

During rehearsals, every time Harrison would turn his back I'd jump up on the stage under the pretense of rehearsing as M.C. for a number and I'd make the band move. The sound was so different when I directed the band that it was almost embarrassing. I could bring out the various sections, highlight the soloists, and make the band lively and vital. Even Harrison knew how much better the band sounded, and after a while wouldn't even bother to come up on the stage during rehearsals. He just let me put the group through its paces, and the next thing he knew, he was out of a job. Like a lot of Negro bands during that time, the Alabamians were a cooperative. The band was owned and run by its members, democratically. They split the fees and the income evenly among themselves, and they made decisions about gigs and management jointly. So when these guys saw what a difference it made to have me conducting, they said, "Hell, this guy should be leading the band," and they voted Harrison out and me in. Just like that.

All of a sudden I had a band of my own, and I went stone crazy. I worked with these guys day and night. We rehearsed every day and played every night. I forgot all about school. To hell with school, I said. I had a chance to make it with a band of my own. And I was still emceeing the revue as well. It was a lot of work, but it was easy because it seemed so natural. It was exactly what I wanted to be doing.

I stayed with the Alabamians for a year. We really developed there, at the Sunset Cafe. We had three saxophones, three trumpets, a trombone, a bass fiddle, drums, a guitar, and a piano. The main writer, arranger, and composer was a sax player named Warren Hardy. He was a bitch. We were playing all the old 1920s jazz and pop tunes—"Tiger Rag," "Jazz Me Blues," "Royal Garden Blues," W.C. Handy's "St. Louis Blues," his "Beale Street Blues," and Louis Armstrong's "Gut-Bucket Blues." In addition, we developed a style of novelty arrangement in which the band members all had megaphones, and I would sing a line and they would hold up their megaphones and respond. The crowds loved our jumping, jiving style, and the dance floor at the Sunset was always hopping.

A few months after I took over as leader, Harry Voiler, who had bought the Sunset Cafe from Joe Glaser, decided to change bands. It was the custom in those days in a club like the Sunset to rotate bands regularly for a change of pace. Voiler came over to me one day and told me he was going to make the change. "But, Cab," he said, "I want you to stay at the Sunset to emcee and help handle the new band that's coming in." I thought about it for a minute. I thought about the great time I was having with the Alabamians—the fact is, I had gone nuts behind conducting this band—and I told him, "No, Harry, I'm sorry. The Alabamians are my band. I'm staying with them."

We were about to leave the Sunset to play other clubs in Chicago when Warren Hardy called for a meeting of the band. He told us that the Music Corporation of America was interested in managing us. We were excited as all get out. The Music Corporation of America was the booking agent for many of the major bands at that time. Then Hardy gave us the real news. "And if we go with them, they'll book us on the road for a few months and in September we go to New York City." Man, the guys roared! That was beautiful. There wasn't a jazz musician in the country that didn't dig coming to New York. Everybody cheered and hugged old Hardy and we all went out and got drunk together. We were going to New York!

We'd been hearing for the last few months how Louis Armstrong and Carroll Dickerson were breaking things up at Connie's Inn, about Fletcher Henderson at the Roseland Ballroom, Duke Ellington at the Cotton Club, Charlie Johnson at Small's Paradise, King Oliver's Dixie Syncopators at the Savoy Ballroom, where Chick Webb's combo played during the intermissions, and about the Panamanian composer Luis Russell at the Club Harlem. We all knew about McKinney's Cotton Pickers and Cecil Scott's Bright Boys, and, of course, the fabled New York City music of individual jazzmen like W.C. Handy, Jelly Roll Morton, James P. Johnson, Willie "The Lion" Smith, and Fats Waller. All of these names were more familiar and more respected than white musicians like Paul Whiteman, the so-called King of Jazz. As far as most of us were concerned, he really didn't play jazz despite his famous performance of George Gershwin's *Rhapsody in Blue* in 1924 at Aeolian Hall.

In May of 1929, we left Chicago and went on the road for three months, but all we could think about was our ultimate destination—New York City.

Chapter 5

Fads and Fancy

Chapter Preface

The culture of the 1920s was the first to be heavily influenced by mass media, which was still in its infancy. The sounds of radio captured the public imagination in much the same way television did three decades later. While sales of radios totaled only $2 million in 1920, that number would reach $600 million by 1929 as nearly every American bought a "Radiola" for the princely sum of $75.

Programming in many areas consisted of whatever station owners could cobble together from local talent. Variety programs might feature hog callers, traveling accordionists, and ventriloquists. Farm and stock market reports were interspersed with game shows, trite dramas, and programs about hobbies such as stamp collecting, mahjong, and bridge.

In larger cities the parade and subsequent hysteria concerning Lindbergh's solo transatlantic flight filled hours of airtime, as did coverage of fads such as dance marathons and flagpole-sitting contests.

Movies also had a unifying force on the American public. For seven cents a patron could spend all day sitting in the plush seat of a luxurious movie palace surrounded by friends, relatives, and neighbors.

On Saturday afternoons, entire towns would flock to shows that included a drama, a comedy or cowboy film, a short subject, one short installment of a twenty-episode mystery—all silent films backed by pianists or organists playing classical music. After the movies ended, shows might include up to ten live vaudeville acts with singers, dancers, jugglers, comedy, and animal acts.

The radio and movies brought Americans together and helped make the world seem a smaller place as entire communities listened to the same events, the same shows, and the same news for the first time in history.

The Glamour and Vulgarity of Hollywood

R.E. Sherwood

By the 1920s the grandiose films of Hollywood were influencing peoples' fashion and behavior across the globe. With perceived powers greater than preachers and presidents, the film capital of the world became a legend in its own right. As an occasional screenwriter, and an editor and motion picture critic for *Life* magazine, R.E. Sherwood was in a unique position to dispel the myths of Hollywood and its glamorous citizens and explain the often boring reality of life in that California city.

There are no lovely legends connected with the origin of that vague section of Los Angeles County which has become the film capital of the world, the most loudly advertised and the most thoroughly misunderstood of all the communities in creation. . . .

However, it is idle to concoct any more myths relating to Hollywood. The place is already effectually obscured by . . . fable. No one, not even those who profess to have solved and mastered its mysteries, has really the faintest notion as to what it is or what it means.

It is, of course, a town, with its quota of newspapers, shops and hotels, its baseball team and athletic club, its banks . . . its Chamber of Commerce and its civic pride. But it is not as

Excerpted from "Hollywood: The Blessed and Cursed," by R.E. Sherwood, in *America as Americans See It,* edited by Fred J. Ringel (New York: Harcourt Brace, 1932).

a town, a paltry dot on the map of California, that it exists in the imagination of mankind; it is an idea—glamorous, insane, alluring or wildly ridiculous, but always tremendously important and fantastically unreal.

You may regard Hollywood as the blessed realm of dreams come true, or as civilization's worst nightmare; but you can hardly afford to ignore it or the inestimable influence that it has exerted. Ten thousand recording angels, working night and day throughout infinity, could not begin to tabulate the volume of laughter and tears and sexual excitation that Hollywood has provoked among the varied races of this earth. (The story is told of the chieftain of a tribe in the depths of Africa who sent an order to the United States for a gleaming white barber's chair, for use as a throne, explaining that he had seen one like it in an Adolphe Menjou picture.)

Undoubtedly, Hollywood's influence is now waning, and it may in time largely disappear. The language barriers that have been discovered since the outburst of sound upon the once-silent screen have naturally narrowed the field for English-speaking film actors. The citadel of the cinema may crumble into dust, as Babylon crumbled in so many of the early celluloid allegories. But . . . I believe that, whatever befalls, the world will not soon be able to obliterate the effects that have been produced on it by such as Greta Garbo, Charles Spencer Chaplin, Mary Pickford and Rudolph Valentino.

An International City

In these four names, surely the greatest that have been promoted in the cinema, may be found at least a partial explanation of the universality of Hollywood's fame. For they point to the fact that the American movie may be counted a manifestation of what we fondly call the American genius only in so far as it is thoroughly hybrid. Miss Garbo, as you all know, came unheralded from Sweden; Mr. Chaplin originated in the east end of London, and Miss Pickford in the province of Ontario [Canada]; the late Mr. Valentino emigrated from Italy to practice the art of landscape gardening. Add to these the names of Ernst Lubitsch, Pola Negri, Ramon Novarro, Marlene Dietrich, George Arliss, Maurice Chevalier, Anna May Wong, Lily Damita, Josef von Sternberg, Norma Shearer, Emil Jannings, Ronald Colman, Sessue Hayakawa, Vilma Banky, Lewis Milestone—as well as [studio heads] Adolph Zukor, William Fox, Carl Laemmle, Samuel Goldwyn—and you have a conception of the cosmopolitanism of the cinema. Geneva [Switzerland] itself could not be more international in its flavor than is Hollywood, where you will observe an impoverished son of the Hungarian nobility eagerly seeking employment from a graduate of a Polish ghetto, or an officer of the [French] Legion of Honor obediently following the directions of an ex-private of the Landsturm [German army].

Whether they liked it or not, the Lords of Hollywood have been shackled by the consciousness of the world market. They have been servants not only of 120,000,000 U.S. citizens, but of the entire human race. (In prosperous times, the greater American film corporations depended upon the foreign trade for as much as half of their total earnings.) One might well imagine that the vastness of their domain would give to the movie people a comforting sense of power, and many of their recorded statements have indeed betrayed a deplorable though reasonable lack of humility. But whatever they say, or whatever their masses of statistics may prove, they know that the very universality of the cinema has been the principal obstacle to its progress. Hollywood has discovered again and again that all the races, and even all the parishes, have patriotic sensibilities which must not be offended. If a picture has a Spanish villain, the rich Central and South American markets are closed to it. If it has a palpably British villain, it will never be passed by the censors in Canada and Australia. (The British Dominions, by the way, are far more sensitive in this respect than is England herself.) And a picture which deals with honest gangsterism or with corruption in municipal government will not be permitted to reach any of the screens in Chicago.

You learn in Hollywood that when you're talking to hundreds of millions of assorted cretins you can't say much.

This is by all odds the most important factor in any consideration of Hollywood. When one gains a glimmering of an understanding of the magnitude of that monster, the world audience, one finds it easier to forgive the movie people for their wild, absurd extravagances, their laughable gaucheries and the manifold artistic crimes that they commit. Imagine the plight of a Hollywood heroine, a not too complex cutie who has been boosted suddenly to dizzy eminence and is rather puzzled by it all: she awakens in the night with the realization, "At this moment I am being subjected to vicarious rape by countless hordes of Jugo-Slavs, Peruvians, Burmese, Abyssinians, Kurds, Latvians and Ku Klux Klansmen!" Is it any wonder that a girl in this predicament finds it difficult to lead a sane, normal life, that her sense of balance is apt to be a bit erratic? But let us depart from these horrid thoughts and examine some historical data.

The First Films

The discovery of Hollywood, like most epoch-making discoveries, was accidental. It happened that, in 1912, Jesse L. Lasky, a vaudeville magnate, joined with his brother-in-law, Samuel Goldfisch, a glove salesman, in the formation of a motion picture producing company. Their first offering (and, they assured themselves, probably their last) was to be "The Squaw Man." They engaged Cecil B. DeMille as director and Dustin Farnum as star, and sent them to Flagstaff, Arizona, to make the picture. Flagstaff was selected because it sounded as though it would provide suitable backgrounds for the enactment of a vigorous Western melodrama, but when DeMille and Farnum arrived there, and took one look at the prospect from the station platform, they stepped back on the train and continued on to the Pacific Coast. A chance acquaintance happened to mention to them a hamlet called Hollywood, a sleepy suburb of Los Angeles, which is itself the largest suburb on earth, and they made that their objective. They rented a barn on Vine Street, and there produced

"The Squaw Man," the first feature picture to be born beneath the California sun.

(I do not know whether there was actually any holly in Hollywood when the first adventurers arrived there, or whether that Christmassy, Dickensian name emerged from the imagination of some pioneer realtor. There is no holly in Hollywood now, nor any green thing that grows by the will of God as opposed to the artifice of man. The water which irrigates the gaudy gardens about the villas of the stars is imported from far distant sources, just as is the supply of talent, ingenuity and sex appeal which animates the cameras.)

After "The Squaw Man" came the first of the immortal Keystone comedies, produced by Mack Sennett, with Ford Sterling, Chester Conklin, Mabel Normand, Fatty Arbuckle, Marie Dressler and, eventually, Charlie Chaplin; then Adolph Zukor moved his Famous Players organization to Los Angeles to make "Tess of the Storm Country," starring little Mary Pickford, and David Wark Griffith arrived with his company of Biograph players to produce the first of the epics, "The Birth of a Nation." In the year 1915, the second gold rush to California assumed colossal proportions.

Broken Dreams

As vast prosperity came to Hollywood, so did scandal, and with it, fame unbounded. The sensational stories, printed in the less scrupulous newspapers and magazines, of Byzantine orgies in the film colony—stories of immorality on the grand scale—conveyed to the avid public the assurance that life in Hollywood was a veritable bed of orchids to be shared with the most desirable, the most god-like representatives of the opposite sex. As a direct result of this lovely misconception, Hollywood became the goal toward which traveled the hopes and dreams of all the frustrated morons: it was recognized as the fountainhead of romance, wherein the frailest, pimpliest ribbon clerk could be converted into a devastating Don Juan and the sorriest slavey [domestic servant] into a voluptuous Cleopatra.

So the highways across the Mojave Desert were clogged with immigrants, following with pathetic confidence the path of the blistering sun, seeking the thing (whatever it was) that had been gained with apparent ease by such bewildering beings as Gloria Swanson, Richard Barthelmess, Clara Bow and Jackie Coogan. Some few of the hundreds of thousands of unsolicited immigrants had been provident enough to bring with them funds sufficient for their support for a week or so in California; others were positive that they had only to knock once upon the studio portals to achieve the miracle of recognition.

The enormous increase in population thus promoted in the Los Angeles district was naturally gratifying to the Chamber of Commerce boosters, but it imposed a terrific strain upon the local charitable organizations. The swarms of candidates for fame and fortune became public charges and consequently damned nuisances. The employees of the Young Men's and Young Women's Christian and Hebrew Associations, the Salvation Army, the Motion Picture Relief Fund, etc., were constantly having to listen to the same sad tale: "I've come all the way from New Bedford (or Quito, or Maida Vale, or Eisenach) and they told me at the studios 'No Casting Today' but if you can only help me out until tomorrow I *know* I'll get a break!"

The break always came, but it was usually in the form of a compound fracture of the illusions. Probably no more than one-fifth of one per cent of those who have journeyed to Hollywood in quest of employment have ever managed to earn a bare living out of the movies.

It must be said for the regular inhabitants of Hollywood that they have done all they could to correct the appallingly false impression of their adopted home town. They were embarrassed and horrified by the stories of fancy vice that were being circulated by gossipy journalists. They believed (erroneously) that this sort of notoriety would hurt their business. Through the offices of the film czar, Will H. Hays, and of that impressively named organization, the Motion Picture Academy of Arts and Sciences, propaganda was spread to persuade mankind that Hollywood was [not a decadent paradise], but, in reality, a reputable community of church-going, God-fearing, temperate, and commendably sexless Puritans.

So effective was this propaganda that the great westward migration diminished appreciably, and so did attendance at all the film theatres. The scandal may have been malicious, and it may have been a distillation of black lies, but it was awfully, awfully good for the box-office.

Exceptionally Pleasant People

What is the real truth about Hollywood? Who am I to tell it?

I have been there in various capacities—as a wide-eyed tourist, as a prying press correspondent and as a writer of lines for talking pictures. I saw the place in the magnificent days of its infancy, and in the later days of its economic decadence; and what I saw was insufficient to inspire me to any rhapsodies of enthusiasm, or blasts of scorn, or bellowings of rage. I found it a dull, ugly, but healthy place, in which the normal problems of life have been simplified to a delightful extent. Liquor is easily obtainable, due to the proximity of the Mexican border, and so is love, due to the constant and overwhelming supply of eager blondes. The toilers in the movie vineyards are exceptionally pleasant people (and this includes even the prominent ones). They are the best of hosts, the best of golfing, gambling, swimming, dancing or drinking companions. They read books, they know what is going on in the world; the great majority of them take neither themselves nor their work with any great degree of seriousness. They are inclined to be self-consciously diffident rather than blatantly boastful, as their chroniclers so often represent them.

The corporate intelligence of Hollywood is not nearly so comical as is supposed by satirists who have never been there. The low cultural level of the cinema is not to be blamed upon the stupidity of those who create it, but upon their complete and not unreasonable contempt for their patrons, the fans, the dreary millions to whom so much reference has been made. "What's the use of trying to be artistic?" the film folk justifiably enquire. "If we give them anything really good, they don't understand it. The only thing that isn't over their heads is Sex."

It is this unshakable conviction which deadens Hollywood, which converts it from the Athens that it might be into the magnified Gopher Prairie that it is. Every writer or actor or artist of any kind who journeys there, however high his hopes or firm his integrity, is bound eventually to arrive at the point where he must utter the same unanswerable question: "What's the use?" And having done so, he must either depart at once, before the California climate dissolves the tissues of his conscience, or he must abandon his idealistic pretensions, settle down to a monotonous diet of the succulent fruits of the lotus, and live out his days, in sun-kissed contentment, accomplishing nothing of any enduring importance, taking the immediate cash and letting the eternal credit go.

Lessons Learned from the Movies

Anonymous

Prior to World War I, movies were considered cheap entertainment for the working class. As the motion picture industry
expanded in the 1920s, however, it began to produce epic
films with glamorous stars such as Rudolph Valentino, Greta
Garbo, and others. By the mid-1920s, 35 million Americans
were attending the movies at least once a week. And the
allure and enchantment of the silver screen was responsible
for fueling fashion fads among young women. In the following excerpt, an unnamed twenty-two-year-old college senior
discusses the effect movies had on her life to renowned
sociologist and author Herbert Blumer.

My real interest in motion pictures showed itself when
I was in about fourth grade at grammar school. There
was a theater on the route by which I went home from
school and as the picture changed every other day I used to
spend the majority of my time there. A gang of us little tots
went regularly.

One day I went to see Viola Dana in *The Five Dollar
Baby.* The scenes which showed her as a baby fascinated me
so that I stayed to see it over four times. I forgot home, dinner, and everything. About eight o'clock mother came after
me—frantically searching the theater.

Next to pictures about children, I loved serials and pie-
throwing comedies, not to say cowboy 'n' Indian stories.

Excerpts from an anonymous college student's "Motion Picture Autobiography,"
in *Movies and Conduct,* by Herbert Blumer (New York, n.p., 1933).

These kind I liked until I was twelve or thirteen; then I lost interest in that type, and the spectacular, beautifully decorated scenes took my eye. Stories of dancers and stage life I loved. Next, mystery plays thrilled me and one never slipped by me. At fifteen I liked stories of modern youth; the gorgeous clothes and settings fascinated me.

My first favorite was Norma Talmadge. I liked her because I saw her in a picture where she wore ruffly hoop-skirts which greatly attracted me. My favorites have always been among the women; the only men stars I've ever been interested in are Tom Mix, Doug Fairbanks and Thomas Meighan, also Doug McLean and Bill Haines. Colleen Moore I liked for a while, but now her haircut annoys me. My present favorites are rather numerous: Joan Crawford, Billie Dove, Sue Carol, Louise Brooks, and Norma Shearer. I nearly forgot about Barbara LaMar. I really worshiped her. I can remember how I diligently tried to draw every gown she wore on the screen and how broken-hearted I was when she died. You would have thought my best friend had passed away.

Why I like my favorites? I like Joan Crawford because she is so modern, so young, and so vivacious! Billie Dove is so beautifully beautiful that she just gets under your skin. She is the most beautiful woman on the screen! Sue Carol is cute 'n' peppy. Louise Brooks has her assets, those being legs 'n' a clever hair-cut. Norma Shearer wears the kind of clothes I like and is a clever actress.

I nearly always have gone and yet go to the theater with someone. I hate to go alone as it is more enjoyable to have someone to discuss the picture with. Now I go with a bunch of girls or on a date with girls and boys or with one fellow.

Day-Dreams and Nightmares

The day-dreams instigated by the movies consist of clothes, ideas on furnishings, and manners. I don't day-dream much. I am more concerned with materialistic things and realisms. Nevertheless it is hard for any girl not to imagine herself cuddled up in some voluptuous ermine wrap, etc.

The influence of movies on my play as a child—all that I remember is that we immediately enacted the parts interesting us most. And for weeks I would attempt to do what that character would have done until we saw another movie and some other hero or heroine won us over.

I'm always at the mercy of the actor at a movie. I feel nearly every emotion he portrays and forget that anything else is on earth. I was so horrified during *The Phantom of the Opera* when Lon Chaney removed his mask, revealing that hideous face, that until my last day I shall never forget it.

I am deeply impressed, however, by pathos [suffering] and pitifulness, if you understand. I remember one time seeing a movie about an awful fire. I was terrified by the reality of it and for several nights I was afraid to go to sleep for fear of a fire and even placed my hat and coat near by in case it was necessary to make a hasty exit. Pictures of robbery and floods have affected my behavior the same way. Have I ever cried at pictures? Cried! I've practically dissolved myself many a time. How people can witness a heart-rending picture and not weep buckets of tears is more than I can understand. *The Singing Fool, The Iron Mask, Seventh Heaven, Our Dancing Daughters,* and other pictures I saw when very young which centered about the death of someone's baby and showed how the big sister insisted on her jazz 'n' whoopee regardless of the baby or not—these nearly killed me. Something like that, anyway; and I hated that girl so I wanted to walk up to the screen and tear her up! As for liking to cry—why, I never thought of that. It isn't a matter of liking or not. Sometimes it just can't be helped. Movies do change my moods, but they never last long. I'm off on something else before I know it. If I see a dull or morose show, it sort of deadens me and the vim and vigor dies out 'til the movie is forgotten. For example, Mary Pickford's movie—*Sparrows*—gave me the blues for a week or so, as did li'l Sonny Boy in *The Singing Fool.* The poor kid's a joke now.

This modern knee-jiggling, hand-clapping effect used for accompanying popular music has been imitated from the movies, I think. But unless I've unconsciously picked up little mannerisms, I can think of no one that I've tried to imitate.

Learning About Love

Goodness knows, you learn plenty about love from the movies. That's their long run; you learn more from actual experience, though! You do see how the gold-digger systematically gets the poor fish in tow. You see how the sleek-haired, long-earringed, languid-eyed siren lands the men. You meet the flapper, the good girl, 'n' all the feminine types and their little tricks of the trade. We pick up their snappy comebacks which are most handy when dispensing with an unwanted suitor, a too ardent one, too backward one, etc. And believe me, they observe and remember, too.

I can remember when we all nudged one another and giggled at the last close-up in a movie. I recall when during the same sort of close-up when the boy friend squeezes your arm and looks soulfully at you. Oh, it's lotsa fun! No, I never fell in love with my movie idol. When I don't know a person really, when I know I'll never have a chance with 'em, I don't bother pining away over them and writing them idiotic letters as some girls I've known do. I have imagined playing with a movie hero many times though; that is while I'm watching the picture. I forget about it when I'm outside the theater. Buddy Rogers and Rudy Valentino have kissed me oodles of times, but they don't know it. God bless 'em!

Yes, love scenes have thrilled me and have made me more receptive to love. I was going with a fellow whom I liked as a playmate, so to speak; he was a little younger than me and he liked me a great deal. We went to the movie—Billie Dove in it. Oh, I can't recall the name but Antonio Moreno was the lead, and there were some lovely scenes which just got me all hot 'n' bothered. After the movie we went for a ride 'n' parked along the lake; it was a gorgeous night. Well, I just melted (as it were) in his arms, making him believe I loved him, which I didn't. I sort of came to, but I promised to go steady with him. I went with him 'til I couldn't bear the sight of him. Such trouble I had trying to get rid of him, and yet not hurt his feelings, as I had led him to believe I cared more than I did. I've wished many times that we'd never seen the movie. Another thing not exactly on the subject but important, I began smoking after watching Dolores Costello, I believe it was, smoke, which hasn't added any joy to my parents' lives.

Lucky Lindy Lands in Paris

Charles A. Lindbergh

When twenty-five-year-old pilot Charles A. Lindbergh achieved the first nonstop solo transatlantic flight from New York to Paris he was completely surprised by the near-hysterical reaction he received when he finally landed in France on May 20, 1927, after more than thirty-three hours of flying. In his autobiography Lindbergh describes the last tense moments of the journey when he was still unsure whether he had even reached Paris's Le Bourget Airport.

Only the lights of small towns and country homes break the blackness of the earth. I turn back on my course, throttle down slightly, and begin a slow descent.

The altimeter shows two thousand feet when I approach the lights again. Close to a large city in an unknown country, it's best not to fly too low. There may be hills with high radio towers on top of them. There are bound to be radio towers somewhere around Paris. I point my pocket flashlight toward the ground, and key out a message. There's no response.

I circle. Yes, it's definitely an airport. I see part of a concrete apron in front of a large, half-open door. But is it Le Bourget [the airport where I wanted to land]? Well, at least it's a Paris airport. That's the important thing. It's Paris I set out for. If I land on the wrong field, it won't be too serious an error—as long as I land safely. I look around once

Excerpted from *The Spirit of St. Louis,* by Charles A. Lindbergh. Copyright © 1953 by Charles Scribner's Sons; copyright renewed 1981 by Anne Morrow Lindbergh. Reprinted with permission of Scribner, a division of Simon & Schuster, Inc.

more for other floodlights or a beacon. There are none—nothing even worth flying over to investigate. I spiral lower, left wing down, keeping close to the edge of the field. There aren't likely to be any radio towers nearby. I'll give those lights along the southern border a wide berth when I come in to land. There may be high factory chimneys rising among them.

From each changed angle, as I bank, new details emerge from night and shadow. I see the corners of big hangars, now outlined vaguely, near the floodlights—a line of them. And now, from the far side of the field, I see that all those smaller lights are automobiles, not factory windows. They seem to be blocked in traffic, on a road behind the hangars. It's a huge airport. The floodlights show only a small corner. It *must* be Le Bourget.

I'll drag [view] the field from low altitude to make sure its surface is clear—that no hay-making machinery, cattle, sheep, or obstruction flags are in the way. After that, everyone down there will know I want to land. If they have any more lights, they'll switch them on. I shift fuel valves to the center wing-tank, sweep my flashlight over the instrument board in a final check, fasten my safety belt, and nose the *Spirit of St. Louis* down into a gradually descending spiral.

Taking a Chance

I circle several times while I lose altitude, trying to penetrate the shadows from different vantage points, getting the lay of the land as well as I can in darkness. At one thousand feet I discover the wind sock, dimly lighted, on top of some building. It's bulged, but far from stiff. That means a gentle, constant wind, not over ten or fifteen miles an hour. My landing direction will be over the floodlights, angling away from the hangar line. Why circle any longer? That's all the information I need. No matter how hard I try, my eyes can't penetrate the blanket of night over the central portion of the field.

I straighten out my wings and let the throttled engine drag me on beyond the leeward border. Now the steep bank into wind, and the dive toward ground. But how strange it is, this descent. I'm wide awake, but the feel of my plane has not returned. Then I must hold excess speed—take no chance of stalling or of the engine loading up. My movements are mechanical, uncoordinated, as though I were coming down at the end of my first solo.

I point the nose just short of the floodlights, throttle half open, flattening out slightly as I approach. I see the whole outline of the hangars, now. Two or three planes are resting in the shadows. There's no time to look for more details. The lighted area is just ahead. It's barely large enough to land on. I nose down below the hangar roofs, so low that

Charles A. Lindbergh

I can see the texture of the sod, and blades of grass on high spots. The ground is smooth and solid as far as the floodlights show its surface. I can tell nothing about the black mass beyond. But those several pin points in the distance look as though they mark the far border. Since Le Bourget is a major airport, the area between is probably also clear— I'll have to take a chance on that; if I land short, I may stop rolling before I reach it.

I open the throttle and start a climbing turn. I don't dare pull the nose up steeply. I don't dare chandelle around the hangars to celebrate my arrival, as I often do coming in with the night mail at Chicago. I must handle the *Spirit of St. Louis* as I'd teach a student to fly.

I climb to a thousand feet. There are the lamps of Paris again, like a lake of stars. There's the dark area below, just as it was before. No one has turned on more lights. I level off for the downwind stretch. The wind sock hasn't changed—still bulged and angling across the line of hangars. The motorcars are still jammed in traffic. There's no sign of movement on the ground.

I'm a quarter-mile downwind now – – – Back on throttle – – – Bank around for final glide. Is my nose down far enough? Yes, the air speed's at ninety miles an hour. I'll overshoot if I keep on at this rate – – – Stick back – – – trim the stabilizer back another notch – – – close the throttle – – – I can hardly hear the engine idling—is it too slow?—It mustn't stop now—The silence is like vacuum in my ears. I open the throttle for a quick burst—But I'm going much too fast.

Running People

In spite of my speed, the *Spirit of St. Louis* seems about to stall. My lack of feel alarms me. I've never tried to land a plane without feel before. I want to open the throttle wider, to glide faster, to tauten the controls still more. But—I glance at the dial—the needle points to eighty miles an hour. The *Spirit of St. Louis* is lightly loaded, with most of its fuel gone. Even at this speed I'll overshoot the lighted area before my tail skid strikes the ground. No, I'll have to pull the nose higher instead of pushing it down. I'll have to depend on the needle, on judgment more than instinct. I kick rudder and push the stick to one side, just to be sure—yes, controls are taut, there's plenty of speed. And feeling is not completely gone. I still have a little left. I can feel the skid and slip. But the edge of perception is dull, very dull. It's better to come in fast, even if I roll into that black area after I land. And it's better to come in high—there may be poles or chimneys at the field's edge—Never depend on obstruction lights—especially when you don't see any.

It's only a hundred yards to the hangars now—solid forms emerging from the night. I'm too high—too fast. Drop wing—left rudder—sideslip – – – Careful—mustn't get anywhere near the stall. I've never landed the *Spirit of St. Louis* at night before. It would be better to come in straight. But if I don't sideslip, I'll be too high over the boundary to touch my wheels in the area of light. That would mean circling again – – – Still too high. I push the stick over to a steeper slip, leaving the nose well down – – – Below the hangar roofs now – – – straighten out – – – A short burst of the engine – – – Over the lighted area – – – Sod coming up to meet me – – – Deceptive high lights and shadows—Careful—easy to bounce when you're tired – – – Still too fast – – – Tail too high – – – Hold off – – – Hold off – – – But the lights are far behind – – – The surface dims – – – Texture of sod is gone – – – Ahead, there's nothing but night – – – Give her the gun and climb for another try? – – – The wheels touch gently—off again—No, I'll keep contact—Ease the stick forward – – – Back on the ground—Off—Back—the tail skid too – – – Not a bad landing, but I'm beyond the light—can't see anything ahead—Like flying in fog—Ground loop?—No, still rolling too fast—might blow a tire—The field *must* be clear—Uncomfortable though, jolting into blackness—Wish I had a wing light—but too heavy on the take-off – – – Slower, now – – – slow enough to ground loop safely—left rudder—reverse it—stick over the other way – – – The *Spirit of St. Louis* swings around and stops rolling, resting on the solidness of earth, in the center of Le Bourget.

I start to taxi back toward the floodlights and hangars – – – But the entire field ahead is covered with running figures!

Unprepared for the Welcome

My reception by the French people . . . cannot be compressed into . . . this book. . . . I was completely unprepared for the welcome which awaited me on Le Bourget. I had no idea that my plane had been so accurately reported along its route between Ireland and the capital of France—over Dingle Bay, over Plymouth, over Cherbourg. When I circled the aerodrome it did not occur to me that any connection existed between my arrival and the cars stalled in traffic on the roads. When my wheels touched earth, I had no way of knowing that tens of thousands of men and women were breaking down fences and flooding past guards.

I had barely cut the engine switch when the first people reached my cockpit. Within seconds my open windows were blocked with faces. My name was called out over and over again, in accents strange to my ears—on this side of my plane—on that side—in front—in the distance. I could feel the *Spirit of St. Louis* tremble with the pressure of the crowd. I heard the crack of wood behind me when someone leaned too heavily against a fairing strip. Then a second strip snapped, and a third, and there was the sound of tearing fabric. That meant souvenir hunters were going wild. It was es-

Lindbergh Accentuates the Positive

High-flying praise for Charles A. Lindbergh's thirty-three-hour journey across the Atlantic poured out from radios, movies, and magazines. In the following excerpt, originally published in the October 1927 issue of the American Magazine, *journalist Mary B. Mullett explains why Americans were so eager to celebrate Lindbergh's record-setting accomplishment.*

Ever since the war there has been an outcry against "modern" character, ideals, and morals; especially against those of the younger generation. Most of us have contributed our share to this chorus of denunciation. All of us have had to listen to it. . . . [But Lindbergh] has shown us that this talk was nothing *but* talk! He has shown us that we are *not* rotten at the core, but morally sound and sweet and good!

At the time Lindbergh made his flight, a particularly atrocious murder was the leading front-page story in the New York newspapers. They were giving columns to it every day. There were other crimes and scandals on the front pages.

Lindbergh banished these to almost complete oblivion. Not exactly that, either. We ourselves banished them! For if

sential to get a guard stationed around my plane before more damage was done.

"Are there any mechanics here?" I asked.

I couldn't understand a single word that came back in answer—from a half-dozen different mouths.

"Does anyone here speak English?" I shouted.

The noise and excitement made a reply impossible. There were rips of fabric every few seconds, and I could feel my tail skid inching back and forth across the ground. I was afraid the *Spirit of St. Louis* might be seriously injured. The thought entered my mind that the longerons would buckle if enough men climbed on top; and I knew the elevators

---

it had not been for the things *we* did, the Lindbergh news would not have demanded much space.

There wouldn't have been much to write about, if there had been no public demonstrations; no parades, dinners, receptions; no tidal wave of letters and telegrams; no truck-loads of gifts; no reams of poetry; no songs; no cheers and shouts; no smiles of pride; no tears of joy; no thrill of possessing, in him, our dream of what *we* really and truly want to be!

When, because of what we believe him to be, we gave Lindbergh the greatest ovation in history, we convicted ourselves of having told a lie *about* ourselves. For we proved that the "things of good report" are the same today as they were nineteen hundred years ago.

We shouted ourselves hoarse. Not because a man had flown across the Atlantic! Not even because he was an American! But because he was as clean in character as he was strong and fine in body; because he put "ethics" above any desire for wealth; because he was as modest as he was courageous; and because—as we now know, beyond any shadow of doubt—*these are the things which we honor most* in life.

To have shown us this truth about ourselves is the biggest thing that Lindbergh has done.

Mary B. Mullett in George E. Mowry, ed., *The Twenties: Fords, Flappers, and Fanatics.* Englewood Cliffs, NJ: Prentice-Hall, 1963.

wouldn't stand much of any pressure without bending. I decided to get out of the cockpit and try to find some English-speaking person who would help me organize a guard to hold back the crowd.

I opened the door, and started to put my foot down onto ground. But dozens of hands took hold of me—my legs, my arms, my body. No one heard the sentences I spoke. I found myself lying in a prostrate position, up on top of the crowd, in the center of an ocean of heads that extended as far out into the darkness as I could see. Then I started to sink down into that ocean, and was buoyed up again. Thousands of voices mingled in a roar. Men were shouting, stumbling. My head and shoulders went down, and up, and down again, and up once more. It was like drowning in a human sea. I lost sight of the *Spirit of St. Louis*. I heard several screams. I was afraid that I would be dropped under the feet of those milling, cheering people; and that after sitting in a cockpit-fixed position for close to thirty-four hours, my muscles would be too stiff to struggle up again.

I tried to sit up – – – to slip down into the crowd – – – to roll over onto my hands and knees. It was useless. I was simply wasting strength that I might need for a final effort to save myself, if my head angled beneath my feet too far. It seemed wisest to relax as much as I could, and let time pass. I realized that the men under me were determined that no matter what happened to them, I would not fall.

After the lapse of minutes whose number I cannot judge, I felt my helmet jerked from my head. Firmer hands gripped on my body. I heard my name more clearly spoken. And suddenly I was standing on my feet—on European ground at last. With arms linked solidly in mine, I began moving slowly, but unnoticed, through the crowd.

"There Is Lindbergh!"

In the week I spent at Paris, between ceremonies and engagements which crammed almost every hour of each day, I pieced together the story of what happened that Saturday night at Le Bourget. Regardless of the skepticism which existed about my flight, the French authorities had prepared for my reception. Extra guards were detailed to the aerodrome; and when reports of my plane being sighted over Ireland, England, and Normandy, brought automobiles pouring out from Paris by the thousands, two companies of soldiers were sent to reinforce the civil police. It was intended that, after I landed, my plane would be guided to a position near the Administration building, where I was to be met by a reception committee of French and American officials. Press photographers and reporters were assigned to appropriate positions.

When the crowd broke down steel fences and rushed out onto the field, all these arrangements collapsed. Police and soldiers were swept away in the rush which followed. Two French aviators—the military pilot Detroyat and the civil pilot Delage—found themselves close to me in the jam of people. Delage grabbed Detroyat's arm and cried, "Come. They will smother him!" Detroyat, being in uniform, and tall, was able to exercise some authority over the men who had me on their shoulders. Once my feet were on the ground, it was too dark for my flying suit to be very noticeable. I soon became an inconspicuous member of the crowd. Meanwhile my helmet had somehow gotten onto the head of an American reporter. Someone had pointed to him and called out, *"There is Lindbergh! There is Lindbergh!"* The crowd had taken over the reporter and left me free.

I might have had difficulty walking when I first tried to step out of the cockpit after landing, but my muscles were well limbered up by the time my feet actually touched French soil. Delage rushed away to get his little Renault car, while Detroyat maneuvered me to the outskirts of the crowd. When the car arrived, I said that before leaving I wanted to be sure a guard had been placed around the *Spirit of St. Louis.* Communication was difficult, because my ears were still deafened from the flight. I spoke no word of French; my new friends, but little English; and in the background were the noises of the crowd. My plane was being taken care of, they told me. I should not try to go back to it. They were determined about that—there was no mistaking their tones and gestures. They laughed and shook their heads as I protested, and kept pointing to the car.

The French Were Mine

We drove into a big hangar, and I was taken to a small room on one side. My friends motioned me to a chair and put out most of the lights—so I would not be discovered by the crowd. Did I need food, drink, the attention of a doctor? Would I like to lie down? they asked. I had only to tell them what I wanted. France was mine, they said. It was easier for me to understand them indoors, with everyone speaking more slowly.

I didn't feel like lying down, and I had no need whatever for a doctor; but I was greatly worried about my plane, even though I received assurances that everything possible was being done to take care of it. I suggested that we drive back out onto the field to make certain, but the two French pilots pursed their lips and shook their heads again. I then asked what customs and immigration formalities I had to go through. I was a little worried about that, since I had no visa. But I received mostly smiles and laughter in reply. I decided that the best thing for me to do was just to wait and let events develop. Was there any word of Nungesser and Coli? I asked. Faces lengthened. No, no news had come.

I remained with Delage while Detroyat went to search for an officer of higher rank. At first, he could find no one. Then, in the midst of the crowd, he came upon Major Weiss of the Bombardment Group of the 34th A.F. Regiment. The Major could not believe that I was sitting in a hangar's darkened room. "It is impossible," he told Detroyat. "Lindbergh has just been carried triumphantly to the official reception committee." Probably he had seen the reporter with my helmet, who had been taken, struggling, to the American Ambassador before the mistake in identity was finally established. But Major Weiss followed Detroyat, and on seeing me insisted that I be taken to his office on the military side of Le Bourget—about a mile away. So we climbed into the Renault again, and drove across the field. Then, it was Major Weiss's turn to go out and search for higher officers.

It must have been an hour later when I heard American voices, and someone said that the Ambassador of the United States was outside. In a moment the door opened, and I was introduced to the Honorable Myron T. Herrick, to his son Parmely, and to his daughter-in-law Agnes. The room soon filled with people.

Full of Gaping Holes

Ambassador Herrick was an extraordinary man. He had a combination of dignity, perception, and kindness, which few in public life possess. After extending a welcome and inquiring about my welfare, which he judged through his eyes more than through my answer, he said he was going to take me back with him to the Embassy. I accepted gladly; but I asked to see the *Spirit of St. Louis* before we left the field.

Ambassador Herrick nodded. "Of course we'll take you to your plane," he said, "if we can get there." A discussion in French followed, with several people taking part. I was assured that it was unnecessary for me to think more about the *Spirit of St. Louis* that night, because it had not been badly damaged, and it had been placed in a locked hangar, under a military guard. I needed to sleep, it was suggested. There would be time enough to see the plane after that.

"Well, how do you feel about it, Captain?" Ambassador Herrick asked.

I couldn't put the cracking wood and ripping fabric from my mind that easily. I was anxious to find out for myself what repairs would have to be made. I didn't know, then, that the French authorities wished to have all repairs completed before I saw my plane. I argued that I wanted to get some items from the cockpit, and to show the mechanics how to put the windows in. Inserting the windows required a special technique, I explained.

After more conversation which I could not understand, we climbed into Delage's car and drove back to the Air-Union hangar which we had left an hour earlier. In the meantime, my *Spirit of St. Louis* had been placed inside. It was a great shock to me to see my plane. The sides of the fuselage were full of gaping holes, and some souvenir hunter had pulled a lubrication fitting right off one of the rocker-arm housings on my engine. But in spite of surface appearances, careful inspection showed that no serious damage had been done. A few hours of work would make my plane air-worthy again.

It was then time for me to rejoin Ambassador Herrick and drive with him to Paris. But my escorts were unable to locate the Ambassador. After hunting for a quarter-hour, they decided to take me to the American Embassy themselves—by a special route to avoid the heavy jam of traffic. So the four of us started out—Weiss, Delage, Detroyat, and I—all in the little Renault. Nobody looked twice at our car as we wound about through the crowd. I settled back in the seat to rest, to see what I could through the window, and to try to understand the English sentences at which my escorts laughed and struggled.

Hours Since I Slept

We traveled over bumpy side roads, toward the outskirts of Paris, stopping once to ask our way. We passed Dugny, Stains, Saint Denis, and entered through the Saint Ouen gate. Soon we were driving between rows of close-packed brick and stone houses with no yards between. It was tremendously different from America. Then came the heart of the city—"Place de l'Opera," Detroyat said. When we reached the end of a long avenue, Delage parked at the curb of a circular area in the center of which was a great stone arch. The surfaces of the arch were sculptured and softly lighted. My friends took me through the arch, and I found myself standing silently with them at the tomb of France's Unknown Soldier, with its ever-burning flame. They wanted my first stop in Paris to be at the Arc de Triomphe, they said.

We arrived at the American Embassy far ahead of Ambassador Herrick. He had searched for me all over Le Bourget. And then his car had become involved in the traffic jam between aerodrome and city. Neither his driver nor his escort of motorcycle police knew about the side roads the French pilots took me over. It was three o'clock when the Ambassador reached his home at No. 2 Avenue d'Iena. I was waiting for him, after eating a supper which his staff very considerately provided in spite of the early hour. By that time a small crowd—mostly newspapermen—had assembled in the street outside. At Herrick's suggestion they were invited in, and I spent a few minutes answering questions and telling them about my flight. Paris clocks marked 4:15 in the morning before I went to bed. It was sixty-three hours since I had slept.

I woke that afternoon, a little stiff but well rested, into a life which could hardly have been more amazing if I had landed on another planet instead of at Paris. The welcome I received at Le Bourget was only a forerunner to the welcome extended by France, by Belgium, by England—and, through messages, by all of Europe. It was a welcome which words of appreciation are incompetent to cover. But the account of my experiences abroad, of my homecoming to the United States, and of my gratitude to the peoples of Europe and America, belongs to a different story.

Flagpole Sitting

Frederick Nelson

Fueled by the rise of radio reporting and tabloid journalism, the Roaring Twenties were a time of fads and foibles. Americans went crazy for dance marathons, a Chinese game called mah-jongg, fashions based on King Tut, and other silly distractions. One of the more inexplicable fads was flagpole sitting, initiated in 1924 by Alvin "Shipwreck" Kelly, a professional stuntman. Kelly's first effort saw him sitting atop a flagpole for 13 hours, 13 minutes, utilizing saddle stirrups to keep himself from falling off while dozing. Later, "Shipwreck" spent 49 days on a flagpole in Atlantic City, New Jersey, with more than 20,000 people watching some portion of the stunt. After Kelly became a national celebrity for his feat, hundreds of others, including dozens of children, attempted to break his record. For reasons unknown, this fad was particularly popular in Baltimore, as journalist Frederick Nelson writes in "The Child Stylites of Baltimore," which appeared in the August 28, 1929, issue of the *New Republic*.

It all started when, a few weeks ago, a curious fellow known as Shipwreck Kelly, who goes about from city to city demonstrating the hardihood of the American posterior by sitting for extended periods on flagpoles, visited the conservative city of Baltimore and "put on a sitting." During his protracted stay aloft, which was long enough to break the world's record for this particular form of virtuosity, Shipwreck attracted large crowds to the park which was the scene of his effort, and the celebration attending his

Excerpted from "The Child Stylites of Baltimore," by Frederick Nelson, *The New Republic*, August 28, 1929. Reprinted by permission of *The New Republic*.

eventual descent was a demonstration of the ease with which almost any form of imbecility becomes important in these States. Inevitably there was a juvenile aspirant to Shipwreck's fame. Boys from time immemorial have wanted to be locomotive engineers, bareback riders, and major generals. Their heroes are, quite naturally, those who cause the most excitement. It was no great surprise, therefore, when one read in the Baltimore newspapers the modest announcement that Avon Foreman, fifteen, had mounted a flagpole and would sit there until he had broken what might be considered the "juvenile record." When he had sat for ten days, ten hours, ten minutes and ten seconds, he decided that the "juvenile record" in this field had been broken, and he came down.

That might have ended the matter had not various people, no longer accounted children, behaved so preposterously. "The older Baltimore" could hardly believe its ears when it learned the details of the hullabaloo following Avon's descent. For days before this amazing event crowds had gathered nightly to see him perched on his platform upon which bright searchlights had been trained by his father, who is an electrician. When Avon decided that his "record" was safe, there was a neighborhood celebration at which Mayor Broening, for whom no occasion lacks its oratorical opportunities, made an address and presented to Avon an autographed testimonial bearing the great seal of Baltimore City. In the course of his remarks the Mayor described Avon's achievement as an exemplification of "the pioneer spirit of early America." It is quite likely His Honor believed it, but it is equally possible that he was merely making a speech. When two or three people are gathered together Mayor Broening makes a speech, and most of his speeches are much the same.

An Exhibition of Grit and Stamina

Whatever these occasional remarks meant to the Mayor, they were a Challenge to the Youth of Baltimore. From that moment Baltimore was dotted with boys and girls ranging

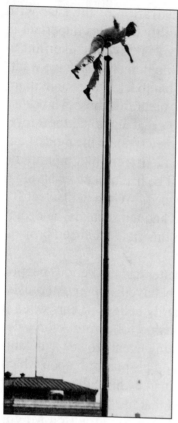

A flagpole sitter demonstrates the popular 1920s fad.

from eight to thirteen years of age who were determined to upset Avon Foreman's record as a flagpole sitter. Some of them came down as soon as Father got home, but since the ceremonies attending the Avon Foreman descent from a flagpole, there has been an average of some fifteen children roosting in various contrivances atop "flagpoles" ranging from ten to twenty feet high. Two of them have broken legs and one an arm, and one little girl was ill for days from the effects of her experience, but others mount poles to replace the casualties and the sittings go on. Parents, who at first were inclined to forbid their youngsters to enter the lists, lend their aid and provide their offspring with such comforts as are possible on top of a pole. It is difficult to make out a case against a practice which the Mayor of a city of 750,000 people has sanctioned as an exhibition of "grit and stamina so essential to success in the great struggle of life."

Editors in Baltimore and elsewhere promptly suggested a quick mobilization of shingles, hairbrushes, straps, and slippers as a means of breaking this children's crusade under the banner of St. Simon Stylites. As a matter of fact, however, the children seem sages in comparison with the imbecility of their elders. When a boy, through the simple expedient of installing himself in a coop at the end of a pole can bring the Mayor to call on him, cause a minister of the

Gospel to hold services with sermon at the foot of the pole and be the central occasion for a brass band, scores of pop-corn vendors, offers of free dentistry for a year and a "write-up" in the newspapers, parental authority—in the class mainly afflicted with this mania—avails very little. Indeed, the parents of most of these children exhibit a distinct pride in the performance, protected by ignorance and stupidity from appreciating the possible consequences, physical and otherwise, of these idiotic vigils. They rival one another in fitting out the child's flagpole equipment with electric lights and, occasionally, a radio set! The corner druggist pays a dollar or two for the right to advertise his business on the sacred totem and the city officials, perhaps in an effort to restrain the epidemic, add importance to flagpole sitting by solemnly issuing specifications for flagpoles for this use and charging a license fee of one dollar! If stripes could cure this malady, other backs than those of the children might appro-priately receive them.

The Thrill of Radio

Graham McNamee

The widespread availability of radios for the first time in the 1920s forever changed American culture. Never before had so many people been able to simultaneously experience sporting events, celebrity fetes, or concerts featuring international stars.

As an announcer for the National Broadcasting Company (NBC) in New York, Graham McNamee was one of the most famous voices in the United States. His enthusiastic, fast-paced descriptions of the World Series, Charles Lindbergh's ticker-tape parade, and other events made him wildly popular among millions of radio listeners.

Broadcasting has come, within the brief ten years of its history, to fill an important function in the public life of America. And this function—a thrilling aspect of radio's place as an entertainment medium—has likewise played an important part in my own career at the microphone.

I refer to our practice in the United States of broadcasting eye-witness reports direct from the scenes of our most spectacular public happenings. Whenever two of our great universities clash in a football game, or a President is inaugurated, or a transatlantic aviator [such as Charles Lindbergh] travels up Broadway to receive one of New York's memorable receptions, the microphone is always there, conveying a word picture of the event to millions of radio sets.

Many times, in the past eight years, it has been my good fortune to be on the "talking end" of those microphones. My job, on the announcing staff of the National Broadcasting

From "Radio Thrills," by Graham McNamee, in *America as Americans See It,* edited by Fred J. Ringel (New York: Harcourt, Brace, 1932).

Company, has been to convey to extensive networks of listeners these verbal descriptions of historic events and pageants—Presidential inaugurations, receptions to returning heroes, mammoth sporting spectacles.

They have been thrilling and unforgettable assignments, despite the fact that they have required a continuous alertness, a tremendous flow of nervous energy, and almost, at times, a capacity for being in many places at once. Special events announcing is a task which demands, above all, a sustained enthusiasm, a fresh and vital interest in the panorama before us. Our reactions to the scene must always be spontaneous and alive—keenly registering the viewpoint of the thousands for whom we are vicarious witnesses.

But as I look back over my memories of the historic events at which I have been radio's reporter, I seem to forget the racked nerves and the drained energy. I remember only the thrills—the excitement—the satisfaction of rubbing elbows with history in the making.

I've probably lost track of a million or so spinal column tingles during my career of special events broadcasting. Enthusiasm, you see, for the pageant or game immediately at hand is my stock in trade. And my spontaneity can't be forced—because my listeners would be the first to recognize it. I just happen to be lucky in that by temperament I'm naturally enthusiastic and excitable.

Friends and listeners frequently ask me, "What has been your greatest thrill at the microphone?" That happens to be an impossible assignment to give my poor memory. For when it comes to discriminating among my thrills, well, I'm like the father of a big family who was asked to name his favorite child, and said simply, "I love them all."

Electrifying Moments

I believe, though, that I can say this: my most electrifying moments have been spent at sporting contests. Even though a baseball or football game exacts a heavy toll in nervous energy, I believe sports have given me my greatest thrills. It brings back the old flush of excitement just to think of some of those moments—Chris Cagle, Army's great backfield star, slashing around tackles for spectacular runs—Frankie Frisch at second base for the New York Giants, scooping up impossible balls and turning them into World Series victories—the procession of those moments still run rampant in my mind's eye.

I think, though, that one of my most thrilling moments occurred during the World Series—America's annual baseball classic—in 1923. Talk about intensity, breath-taking and vivid, packed into a few minutes of dramatic action! The incident I'm thinking of occurred in the sixth game of that series, and the New York Yankees were leading the New York Giants, three games to two. In the eighth inning of this sixth game, the Giants were on the long end of a 4–1 score, and it looked as though they were going to tie the series at three games each. Then came the memorable rally—the unforgettable thrill!

The Yankees, aided by a collapse of the Giants' pitching staff and clean hit by Bob Meusel, drove in four runs, took the lead and won the series. It's difficult to imagine the gripping drama of that situation unless you realize what a tremendous hold our national sport has on the average American. I'm a real patriot, I guess, for I never yet had to "fake" interest in a first class football or baseball game.

But sports announcing is not the only kind of microphone reporting which has color and glamour and makes the heart beat a little faster. The thrills of broadcasting never grow old, because they are so varied.

For example, it's a far cry from one of our gigantic university stadiums, where 100,000 delirious, partisan enthusiasts are watching intercollegiate football, to a dimly lighted, luxuriously draped studio in which a Schumann-Heink or Louise Homer is about to sing. Yet, I get an unforgettable reaction from either situation.

And so my memories run—the historic receptions accorded to Lindbergh and [Antarctic explorer Richard] Byrd—my flight in an airplane, 5,000 feet above New York's Central Park, talking to the radio audience and to

Captain Frank M. Hawks, holder of many American airplane speed records—the inauguration of President Hoover—the championship fights between Jack Dempsey and Gene Tunney—celebrities on intimate parade before my microphone.

Seventy-five football battles, thirty-eight World Series baseball games, a score of championship prize fights, besides all the other special stunts and functions I've witnessed with a microphone at my elbow, haven't dulled me or left me satisfied. In fact, I don't believe I'd change jobs with any one in the world.

Chapter 6

Wall Street Goes Bust

Chapter Preface

When Herbert Hoover ran for president in 1928, he confidently predicted in campaign speeches that the abolition of poverty was right around the corner. The steadily rising bull market in the nine months after his inauguration proved that point to millions of Americans.

Day after day newspaper headlines reported the skyrocketing stock prices of companies such as RCA and General Motors. Values of obscure companies such as Western Warehouses tripled within weeks. Traditional business practices were forgotten as stocks no longer increased in value because the company made money or produced a desirable product.

In September 1929, the market began a roller-coaster ride that made many investors queasy. Stocks would soar to new highs, then lose half their original value within a few days. Meanwhile several large banks had lent brokers over $6 billion (equal to around $330 billion today) so that small investors could buy stocks on margin (with borrowed money). Others set up investment trusts—companies that owned large amounts of stock—and then sold stock in those companies, which were bought by other investment trusts, which then sold stock in those companies.

This financial house of cards came crashing down on October 24, 1929, when the market wiped out a year's worth of gains in one day. By October 29, the market was in free fall and the slide continued for the next several months. By 1932, the Dow Jones Industrial Average had lost 89 percent of its 1928 value, and the United States was in a deep economic depression. More than 25 percent of adults were out of work, and the unparalleled dreams of wealth that buoyed the nation throughout the Roaring Twenties seemed like a cruel joke to the homeless and hungry.

The Day the Bottom Dropped Out

Gordon Thomas and Max Morgan-Witts

> October 24, 1929, will always be remembered as Black
> Thursday on Wall Street. On that day panic swept through
> the New York Stock Exchange as hysterical speculators
> attempted to sell their stocks in a mad rush to get out of the
> market as quickly as possible. Best-selling journalists Gordon
> Thomas and Max Morgan-Witts recreated the panic of that
> day by conducting interviews and utilizing the memoirs, doc-
> uments, and private papers from survivors of the great crash.

Three minutes after ten would remain forever in [W.E.
"Hut" Hutton's] memory as the moment an excited
shout swept through [the brokerage firm]. "She's trading big
and brisk!"

The market had opened "like a bolt out of hell."

Kennecott Copper, which had slumped just before yesterday's close, leaped $11 on a 20,000-share transaction.
Sinclair Oil jumped fifty cents on a 15,000-share deal. Standard Brands rose almost forty cents after a block of 15,000
shares was traded.

Hut moved to the point of greatest need, the trading table,
a huge desk bristling with telephones. His colleagues around
it could not keep up with the calls; every unanswered phone
was ringing. Hut joined in the general scramble. As soon as
a phone was put down, it rang again. The time each call was
received, and its message, was carefully noted.

Many callers begged for an extension of their margin deadlines [money borrowed against stock] now that the market showed signs of reviving. A few were granted extensions; the majority were told the deadlines stood.

At 10:10 a buy order for 13,000 shares of Packard Motors added further hope the market really was in a mood to recover.

For the next fifteen minutes, prices remained generally steady. Apart from the unusually large number of leading stocks changing hands in big blocks, there was no particular pattern or trend to the trading.

Then, at 10:25, a 20,000 block of General Motors showed a loss of eighty cents a share.

Four minutes later, at 10:29, Hut picked up the phone.

In a hysterical voice, desperate to accept any price offered, the caller shrieked a phrase beginning to be heard in brokerage houses throughout the district:

"Sell at the market [price]."

"Expect No Help"

Ten-fifty A.M.—again the moment was fixed in his memory—Pat Bologna achieved what he had been trying to do for the past twenty minutes: force his way into the customers' room close to his pitch. The young shoeblack had his entire savings of $5,000 invested on margin.

The scene Bologna saw was typical of those that would serve as the basis for numerous "eyewitness accounts" written later by journalists. None of them would quite capture the raw impact the room had on Bologna.

"In the crowd there's a Chinaman wearing a hat which rests on his ears. He's got a dead cigar in a mouth of dead teeth. He's standing on tip-toe to see over the shoulders of a woman wearing a big fancy hat. She's holding out her wedding ring and shouting 'you want more margin—you can't have more margin.' He's drunk as a lord. Everybody is shouting. They're all trying to reach the glass booth where the clerks are. Everybody wants to sell out. The boy at the quotation board is running scared. He can't keep up with the speed of the way stocks are dropping. The board's painted green. The guy who runs it is Irish. He's standing at the back of the booth, on the telephone. I can't hear what he's saying. But a guy near me shouts, 'the sonofabitch has sold me out!'"

The remark made Bologna hesitate. He had come to the room expecting to receive help; clearly, in these crazed conditions, that was impossible.

Bologna could not make up his mind whether to sell the stock he held in Charles Mitchell's National City Bank. He recalled the advice the master banker had once given him after he had finished shining his shoes. Mitchell, along with his usual dollar tip, had passed on guidance. "A wise man never sells out at the first sign of trouble. That's for the pikers."

Acting on the multimillionaire's words, Bologna turned and elbowed his way out of the melee. He had decided to retain his holdings a little longer.

Nothing Anyone Could Do

Close to 11:00 A.M., Charles Stewart Mott at his office in Detroit received some unwelcome information. The specialist in General Motors on the New York Exchange had taken a moment away from Post Four to let Mott know there was nothing he could do to stop the company's stock falling.

Nor had there been time for Mott to ask questions or give orders before the long-distance connection was broken.

The tremendous activity in the market was beginning to impose a severe strain on the entire communication network linking Wall Street to the outside world. Brokers whose private wires were already overworked were being forced to fall back on ordinary commercial telegraph lines; in turn, those lines were also becoming clogged with the unaccustomed traffic. The Bell Telephone Company announced it was busier than it had ever been during the previous peak periods of the Great War. Overseas calls doubled.

Mott summoned his executives into emergency session. His secretary was given strict instructions to disturb him only if more news came in from Wall Street.

At about the same time, Thomas Lamont's secretary, on the second floor of 23 Wall, finally got through to Charles Mitchell's offices on the second floor of the National City Bank at 55 Wall. It had taken her almost ten minutes telephonically to connect two offices only one block apart. The switchboards at . . . the bank were almost jammed.

Lamont's secretary inquired whether Mitchell could join a meeting of bankers just after midday, "to exchange information on the stock-market situation."

Mitchell's secretary, having checked, said Mitchell would be pleased to attend.

Panic Prevailing

By 11:30, William Crawford could see that, increasingly, the proprieties of normal Exchange behavior were being disregarded. The rules specifically stated traders should not "run, curse, push or go coatless."

All around him men were doing precisely that. Since eleven o'clock, "panic had prevailed on the Stock Exchange floor—there was no other word for it."

The confusion was compounded by the minute as the ticker [tape machine] lagged further and further behind. No one could tell what the true trading situation was. . . .

Meanwhile, Crawford paced between the four trading stockades closest to his podium.

At Post One—where Borden, Du Pont, Electric Power and Light, St. Paul Railroad, Sinclair Oil, and United Aircraft were traded—floor brokers were literally being pinned against the trading counter by the overwrought throng.

At Post Three—Allegheny, Columbia Gas, Erie Railroad, Macy & Company—the position was equally frenzied.

But the center of "a kind of madness" was Post Two. Everyone there appeared to be "bellowing like a lunatic." The object of their attention was General Oliver Bridgeman, specialist for U.S. Steel. He knew if steel continued to plunge, it could "carry everything else down the chute with it." Bridgeman was surrounded by a waving, roaring rabble. Every so often he would crouch, scribble some figures on a pad, then leap up and shout even louder than the rest as he tried frantically to stop steel's paper value melting before his horrified eyes.

Suddenly, at Post Four—Anaconda, Caterpillar Tractor, Southern Pacific, U.S. Pipe and Foundry, General Motors—Crawford saw "a fat, perspiring man become almost hysterical, yelling orders that made no sense until some friends seized him by the arm and led him away."

The panic had claimed one of its first recorded casualties.

Eleven thirty-five A.M. found Hut yelling into his tele-

Wild Disorder on Wall Street

On October 23, 1929, panic swept across Wall Street as stock prices dropped precipitously. Even the normally staid Associated Press expresses alarm in the following widely published newspaper story that reported the crash.

Wall Street was thrown into the nearest approximation of a stock market panic experienced in years during the last hour of trading on the Stock Exchange today.

A new and wholly unexpected method of selling swept over the market, carrying scores of stocks down and wiping out more than $3,000,000,000 in paper values in the brief interval of about an hour, an average of about $50,000,000 a minute.

Stock price averages and indices indicated that never before in modern financial history had quoted values disappeared so swiftly. Bankers pointed out, however, that in view of the amazing and unprecedented rise in stock prices in the past year and a half, this break could by no means be regarded as reducing prices to disastrously low levels.

The thoroughly demoralizing aspect of the collapse was its swiftness. The market opened rather dull and drifted along, with several important stocks recording temporary gains, until midafternoon, when a sharp bear drive was launched against . . . automotive equipment and radio stocks, several of which were sent down $40 or more to new low levels for the year.

phone for "quotes as of this moment." He was talking to one of W.E. Hutton's clerks on the Exchange floor.

Hut had spoken to the man by phone many times each day since joining the firm; he knew his voice and vocabulary intimately, "though as so often happens in this business, I wouldn't have recognized him if I saw him."

Over the tie line, the clerk always gave the impression of being calm and collected; now, his demeanor had cracked. He sounded "like a kid close to tears."

Hut asked him for quotations for half a dozen shares.

Traders and investors alike were in a highly nervous state of mind owing to the severe decline in prices during the past fortnight, and as soon as the market showed signs of going into a further slump, they rushed to get rid of their stocks for what they would bring.

The trading facilities were completely overwhelmed. The quotations on the ticker tape fell an hour behind the trading, and as word reached Commission House board rooms that stocks were selling several dollars below prices on the tape, traders became thoroughly frightened and sold without rhyme or reason. Total sales of 6,368,300 shares were piled up, of which about 2,600,000 shares changed hands between 2 and 3 o'clock. . . . The ticker did not print the final quotation until an hour and three-quarters after the close. More than 100 shares were carried to new lows for the year.

While brokers acknowledged that thousands of small traders had undoubtedly been completely wiped out, the senior partner of one of the largest commission houses stated that a tremendous amount of stock, having been held over a period of months, was sold at a profit.

There were scenes of wild disorder on the trading floor during the last hour. The market was flooded with selling orders and for a time suffered from a panicky lack of buying orders. Members screeched their offers for several minutes at a time without finding takers.

Associated Press, *Reform, War, and Peace: 1901–1929.* Danbury, CT: Grolier Educational Corporation, 1995.

The clerk wailed. "I can't get them. I can't get any information! The whole place is falling apart!"

It was not so much the words that stunned Hut; it was the tone of utter despondency in the clerk's voice. . . .

"We're Wiped Out"

Six P.M. found Edith Stone hovering between her bedroom and the radio in the living room. Several times during the afternoon she had paused in her writing to listen to the latest bulletin from Wall Street.

The financial district was said to resemble an armed camp, with four hundred policemen on duty. A reporter had broadcast a graphic picture of brokers with sweat pouring down their faces, their collars and shirts torn to shreds. Edith particularly liked one of his phrases—"they were like shell-shocked soldiers, crazily flinging handfuls of torn ticker tape and order pads in the air."

Perhaps her father had been right when he had forbidden her to set foot in the area today.

The latest news report stated that, in spite of the traumatic first three hours of trading, the market had closed on an upward beat. It was said that U.S. Steel had even shown a gain on yesterday's close. There was growing belief the rally would continue tomorrow.

Edith was relieved. Her father had gone to work apprehensive. She suspected yesterday's break had been a bad one for him.

When Edward Stone opened the front door of the apartment, his daughter saw immediately that something was seriously wrong.

She started to move toward him.

"Stop! Stop everything! We've got to move out!"

Frightened by the hysteria in his voice, certain her father was acutely ill, Edith remained still.

Slowly, as if to memorize every detail, Edward Stone's staring eyes scanned the room, taking in the expensive paintings, the new furnishings, the crystal wall lights, the hand-sewn carpets and drapes.

A crowd gathers outside the New York Stock Exchange following Black Thursday. Thousands of investors lost their life savings in the crash of 1929.

Once more his voice broke the silence. "We can't keep any of it. I haven't a penny. The market's crashed. We're wiped out. Nothing!"

Edith gasped. As she turned toward the kitchen and called to her mother, her father lunged past her.

"I'm going to kill myself! It's the only way. You'll have the insurance. . . ."

Screaming, also close to hysteria, Edith chased after her father. Mabel Stone rushed from the kitchen.

"Ed, for God's sake!"

Her husband reached the French doors leading onto the apartment's terrace. They were closed.

It gave Edith and her mother the chance to catch up. Edith grabbed her father around the waist; his wife tried to pull his hands from the door.

He broke their hold, turned the key, and wrenched open the door.

For a moment Edward Stone stood in the doorway. Then, panting, he turned to his wife and daughter.

Edith would never forget how he kept repeating "the same terrible words, he wouldn't stop saying them."

"The money's gone. All of it. We can't get it back. You'll have the insurance. . . ."

"Ed, for God's sake, you have a wife and family . . . !"

"Get back!"

He turned and took hold of the balcony's railing. The street was twenty floors below.

Edith and her mother simultaneously lunged at him. This time Edith did not let go. She hooked both arms around her father's neck and pulled, determined if necessary to choke him into unconsciousness. Mabel Stone tackled her husband around the knees.

The force of their combined assault brought Edward Stone to the floor.

For a moment they were locked in an impasse.

"Please. Listen . . ."

Edith loosened her grip.

It was a mistake. Her father broke his wife's hold on his legs, got away from his daughter, and leaped again to his feet.

"Mama! We've got to stop him! He's going to jump!"

Even as she shouted, Edith managed to get a grasp on his foot. Twisting it savagely, she toppled her father back to the ground.

She dived on him, helping her mother pinion him to the terrace. Edith would remember his eyes bulging, his mouth opening and shutting but now saying nothing, as if driven by compulsion to suicide.

Close to breaking herself, the slimly built Edith knew she could not physically restrain him much longer. She fell back on the only weapon she had: words. "I called him a sissy, yelled at him, reviled him, hated him for what he was making me say and do."

Edward Stone began to cry.

His wife slapped him twice—hard on each cheek.

He whimpered on for some moments. Then he slowly came to his senses.

One of the servants arrived.

Mabel Stone rose to her feet and, in a controlled voice, told him that her husband had suffered a fall.

In silence they led Edward Stone inside. Only there was he able to tell them the facts. He had lost close to $5 million. They would have to fire the staff, move out at once from their new apartment, and completely readjust their lifestyle.

"Ed, it doesn't matter. We'll manage somehow."

Edith thought her mother was the "most magnificent person in the whole rotten world."

Together, she was certain they had saved her father's life. She also knew what had happened would now make it impossible for her to contemplate further any play about Wall Street.

False Assurances

At 7:08 P.M., 248 minutes late, the ticker finally finished recording the day's story. Brokers had traded in 974 different stocks during a Crash which saw 12,894,650 shares change hands—a record.

But the morning's losses of $6 billion had been halved during the afternoon.

It was enough to provide comfort.

After the last stock price had stuttered out, there followed a brief news item.

Representatives of thirty-five of the largest wire houses in Wall Street issued a joint statement saying the market was "fundamentally sound" and "technically in better condition than it has been in months."

The statement ended with four unforgettable words: "The worst has passed."

Business Leaders React to the Crash

William Starr Myers and Walter H. Newton

> To calm people's fears in the weeks after the 1929 stock-market crash, nearly all of America's business, political, and economic leaders offered positive words about the strength of the U.S. economy. Never before have so many experts been so famously wrong. The U.S. economy was about to head into an unprecedented tailspin and the resulting Great Depression would not end for the majority of Americans until the beginning of World War II in 1942.
>
> The following statements were compiled by Walter H. Newton, personal secretary to President Herbert Hoover. He was aided in his task by William Starr Myers, professor of politics at Princeton University.

T he mental unpreparedness among business and economic leaders at the time of the stock crash and their disbelief in the realities of the situation are of interest in establishing the state of public mind generally. The following public statements were partly the result of a genuine attempt to prevent panic and partly the result of a total lack of knowledge and appreciation of the real situation. They are proof that people seldom recognize inflation or its dangers while it is in progress, or even during the first stages of the collapse.

October 22, 1929: Professor Irving Fisher of Yale said: "Even in the present high market the prices of stocks have not caught up with their real values. Yesterday's break was a shaking out of the lunatic fringe that attempts to speculate on margin." During the next few weeks he predicted a "ragged market returning eventually to further steady increases." *October 24th:* Charles E. Mitchell, of the National City Bank of New York: "This reaction had badly outrun itself." *The New York Times* of the same date stated: "Confidence in the soundness of the stock market structure notwithstanding the upheaval of the last few days was voiced last night by bankers and other financial leaders." Thomas W. Lamont, of J.P. Morgan & Co., said: "Prices of many important issues had been carried down below the levels at which they might be fairly expected to sell.". . . *October 29th:* The press generally made optimistic statements. John D. Rockefeller [one of the richest men in the United States] issued a statement asserting conditions were sound and announced that he was buying stocks. *October 30th:* It was too much to expect partisan politics to remain out of the picture. Senator Joseph T. Robinson of Arkansas, the Democratic leader, made the statement that President Hoover was responsible for the crash but said stocks would recover their prices. The Democratic National Committee, over the name of Senator Millard E. Tydings, of Maryland, blamed the President for the stock crash. John J. Raskob, in a statement in *The New York Times,* declared: "Prudent investors are now buying stocks in huge quantities and will profit handsomely when this hysteria is over and our people have opportunity in calmer moments to appreciate the great stability of business by reason of the sound fundamental economic conditions in this great country of ours." Mr. Raskob was asked by an interviewer if he believed that the decline in the stock market would have great effect on business. He answered that he did not believe the effects would be other than temporary, lasting probably two or three months, and that he did not believe that they would be drastic in other than luxury industries. . . .

November 1, 1929: Stuart Chase, popular writer and radical economist, said that "the stock markets will not affect general prosperity." *November 2nd:* Alfred P. Sloan, Jr., president of the General Motors Corporation, stated: "Business is sound." . . . *November 22nd:* William Green, president of the American Federation of Labor, announced: "All the factors which make for a quick and speedy industrial and economic recovery are present and evident. The Federal Reserve System is operating, serving as a barrier against financial demoralization. Within a few months industrial conditions will become normal, confidence and stabilization in industry and finance will be restored." *December 7th:* Again William Green reassured the public: "We are going to move forward until I think in a few months we will be back to a normal state in the industrial and economic life of our nation." *December 8th: The New York Times* stated: "That there has been a distinct change of sentiment on the outlook for business in 1930 during the last month is apparent. The credit for this impression is given by business leaders to plans under way for industrial expansion during the next year, as revealed at the conference called by President Hoover with key men in all lines. Lack of widespread commercial failures, the absence of serious unemployment, and robust recovery in the stock market have been factors calculated to dispel the gloominess which threatened . . . in the country as a result of the market collapse in October and November." *December 23rd: The New York Journal of Commerce* said: "As a matter of fact there is nothing fundamentally unsound as far as can be learned in our present situation."

January 1, 1930: The public expressions of the administration for the new year were reserved but hopeful. Secretary of the Treasury Mellon said: "Forecasting the future course of business can never be done with any certainty. . . . It is hazardous to attempt to do so. . . . I see nothing in the situation which warrants pessimism. . . . There is plenty of credit available." Likewise, Secretary of Commerce Robert P. Lamont said: "It is impossible to forecast what temporary ups and downs may occur . . . but one may predict for the long run a continuance of prosperity and progress."

Sound and Prosperous

President Hoover was still apprehensive of the boom and its consequences. He naturally felt it wise not to discourage the country in so serious a situation by publishing any misgivings. At the same time he steadily refused to be drawn into discussion of the value of stocks. On *October 25th,* in response to the press clamor, the President declined to issue any statement as to the stock market, but said: "The fundamental business of the country, that is, production and distribution, is on a sound and prosperous basis." Treasury officials stated that "the break was the result of undue speculation." On *November 15th* one influential newspaper made a demand that the President urge the people to invest in stocks, with the assurance that they were cheap. The President ignored this editorial demand, for he had no intention to lead the public in the stock market at that or any other time.

The crash soon realized the President's worst and underlying fears in the extent of its damage to business, employment, and agriculture. The first and most urgent problem of the moment was to prevent the development of the stock panic into a general banking panic. Within thirty days securities had shrunk $30,000,000,000 in value. Brokers' loans of almost $8,000,000,000, made mostly to speculators, in two and a half months made a precipitous descent to $3,500,000,000. The persons owing this money of necessity were forced to reduce their bank deposits or to borrow elsewhere. A graphic indication of the shrinkage of business was the fact that bank debits to individual accounts in 141 cities decreased from $95,000,000,000 to $60,000,000,000 in three months, although loans did not decrease.

Chronology

1920

The U.S. population is 106.4 million; average life expectancy is fifty-four years; over 9 million Americans own cars.

January 2: In the "Palmer Raids," Attorney General A. Mitchell Palmer sends federal agents to round up and deport thousands of suspected communists, most of them innocent of any crime.

January 16: The Eighteenth Amendment to the Constitution goes into effect barring the manufacture, sale, or possession of alcoholic beverages.

March 8: The Socialist Party nominates Eugene Debs for presidency although he is in prison as a result of the Red Scare.

August 26: The Nineteenth Amendment, giving women the right to vote, is ratified.

September 8: Airmail service is established between New York and San Francisco.

November 2: Warren G. Harding is elected president.

1921

By the end of the year, women's hemlines climb to knee length and continue to rise.

March 18: A delegation of representatives from Marcus Garvey's Universal Negro Improvement Association arrive in Monrovia, Liberia, to discuss a reconstruction program with the Liberian government.

May 19: Congress cuts foreign immigration by 97 percent; these restrictions remain in place until the 1970s.

October 5: Radio station WJZ in Newark, New Jersey, is the first ever to broadcast a baseball game—the first game of the 1921 World Series.

1922

May 20: The Lincoln Memorial is dedicated in Washington, D.C.

August 28: Radio station WEAF in New York City broadcasts the first commercially sponsored program.

September 4: James H. Dolittle sets a record by flying across the United States in less than twenty-four hours.

1923

The first dance marathons are held.

March 23: The national news magazine *Time* makes its publishing debut.

May 9: A federal judge rules that Prohibition does not limit prescriptions for whiskey written by physicians.

August 2: Warren G. Harding dies unexpectedly from a heart attack; Calvin Coolidge becomes president.

September 15: The activities of the Ku Klux Kan become so violent and threatening in Oklahoma that the governor places the state under martial law.

December 6: Calvin Coolidge gives the first official presidential message on radio.

1924

Alvin "Shipwreck" Kelly starts a national fad by sitting atop a flagpole in Los Angeles for more than thirteen hours.

Membership in the Ku Klux Klan reaches a record high of 4 million people.

June 10: Henry Ford announces the production of his ten millionth car and lowers the price of a Model T to under $290.

June 30: Former Interior Secretary Albert Fall and others are indicated for their role in the Teapot Dome scandal.

November 4: Calvin Coolidge is officially elected president, having served two years after Harding died.

1925

The Great Gatsby by F. Scott Fitzgerald is published.

January 5: In Wyoming, Nellie Tayloe Ross becomes the first woman governor in the United States by completing her deceased husband's term.

July 10: The trial of John T. Scopes begins in Dayton, Tennessee; Scopes will be convicted of breaking a state law that forbids the teaching of evolution.

August 8: Over 30,000 members of the Ku Klux Klan march down Pennsylvania Avenue in Washington, D.C., in the largest Klan parade in history.

1926

Henry Ford revolutionizes the manufacturing business by introducing the eight-hour day and the five-day week for his workers.

March 7: The first transatlantic conversation by telephone is held between New York and London.

May 9: Richard E. Byrd and Floyd Bennett make the first flight over the North Pole.

September 18: A hurricane devastates Florida (killing 372 and wounding 6,000), and effectively ending the land boom.

1927

February 23: Congress creates the Federal Communications Commission to regulate the radio industry.

March 3: The Treasury Department establishes a Prohibition Bureau to fight bootlegging.

May 16: The first Oscars for movie excellence are awarded in Hollywood.

May 20: Charles A. Lindbergh begins his solo transatlantic flight from New York, landing in Paris 33 1/2 hours later.

September 27: New York Yankee Babe Ruth hits his sixtieth home run of the season, setting a record that will stand for over three decades.

October 6: *The Jazz Singer,* the first "talkie" movie, is released in New York and plays to sold-out houses.

December 2: The Model T era comes to an end when Henry Ford introduces the bigger, better—and more expensive—Model A.

1928

June 30: The first color motion picture film is produced by Kodak.

November 6: Herbert Hoover is elected president.

November 16: The New York Stock Exchange reports a record trading of 6.6 million shares.

1929

The U.S. population is 121.7 million, nearly 26.5 million Americans own automobiles.

February 14: The St. Valentine's Day Massacre in Chicago leaves seven members of George "Bugs" Moran's gang dead.

April 4: The New York City police commissioner reports there are at least thirty-two thousand speakeasies in that city.

October 24: Stock prices fall sharply as 13 million shares exchange hands on what becomes known as "Black Thursday."

October 29: On "Black Tuesday" Wall Street faces its worst day in history as 16 million shares are sold and the bottom drops out of the market. Nearly $14 billion of investor money is wiped out as the country slides into the Great Depression.

For Further Research

Jules Abels, *In the Time of Silent Cal*. New York: G.P. Putnam's Sons, 1969.

Frederick Lewis Allen, *Only Yesterday: An Informal History of the Nineteen-Twenties*. New York: Harper & Brothers, 1957.

Associated Press, *Reform, War, and Peace: 1901–1929*. Danbury, CT: Grolier Educational Corporation, 1995.

Loren Baritz, *The Culture of the Twenties*. Indianapolis: Bobbs-Merrill, 1970.

Laurence Bergreen, *Capone: The Man and the Era*. New York: Touchstone, 1994.

James Boylan, ed., *The World and the 20s*. New York: Dial Press, 1973.

Cab Calloway and Bryant Rollins, *Of Minnie the Moocher and Me*. New York: Thomas Y. Crowell, 1976.

Bruce Catton, "The Restless Decade," *American Heritage*, August 1965.

Cultural Shock: Music and Dancing website, "Early Jazz 1900–1930," www.pbs.org/wgbh/cultureshock/flashpoints/music/jazz_at.html, 2000.

Ronald L. Davis, ed., *The Social and Cultural Life of the 1920s*. New York: Holt, Rinehart, and Winston, 1972.

Editors of Time-Life Books, *The Jazz Age: The 20s*. Alexandria, VA: Time-Life, 1998.

Harold U. Faulkner, *From Versailles to the New Deal*. Toronto: Glasgow, Brook, 1950.

Roberta Strauss Feuerlicht, *American's Reign of Terror*. New York: Random House, 1971.

F. Scott Fitzgerald, *The Great Gatsby*. New York: Charles Scribner's Sons, 1925.

J.C. Furnas, *Great Times: An Informal Social History of the United States.* New York: G.P. Putnam's Sons, 1974.

Marcus Garvey, *Marcus Garvey: Life and Lessons.* Eds. Robert A. Hill and Barbara Bair. Berkeley: University of California Press, 1987.

Allen Jenkins, *The Twenties.* New York: Universe Books, 1974.

Peter Jennings and Todd Brewster, *The Century.* New York: Doubleday, 1998.

John Kobler, *Ardent Spirits: The Rise and Fall of Prohibition.* New York: G.P. Putnam's Sons, 1973.

Gerda Lerner, ed., *The Female Experience: An American Documentary.* Indianapolis: Bobbs-Merrill, 1977.

Charles A. Lindbergh, *The Spirit of St. Louis.* New York: Charles Scribner's Sons, 1953.

Leonard Maltin, *The Great American Broadcast: A Celebration of Radio's Golden Age.* New York: Dutton, 1997.

John Margolies and Emily Gwathmey, *Ticket to Paradise: American Movie Theaters and the Fun We Had.* Boston: Little, Brown, 1991.

Andrew Marum and Frank Parise, *Follies and Foibles: A View of 20th Century Fads.* New York: Facts On File, 1984.

Robert S. McElvaine, *The Great Depression: America, 1929–1941.* New York: Times Books, 1984.

Milton Melzer, *Brother Can You Spare a Dime?* New York: Random House, 1969.

Bettina Miller, ed., *From Flappers to Flivers.* Glendale, WI: Reminisce Books, 1995.

Ethan Mordden, *That Jazz! An Idiosyncratic Social History of the American Twenties.* New York: G.P. Putnam's Sons, 1978.

Joe Alex Morris, *What a Year!* New York: Harper & Brothers, 1956.

George E. Mowry, *The Twenties: Fords, Flappers, and Fanatics.* Englewood Cliffs, NJ: Prentice-Hall, 1963.

William Starr Myers and Walter H. Newton, *The Hoover Administration: A Documented Narrative.* New York: Charles Scribner's Sons, 1936.

Eliot Ness and Oscar Fraley, *The Untouchables.* New York: Award Books, 1975.

Michael E. Parrish, *Anxious Decades.* New York: W.W. Norton, 1992.

Fred J. Ringel, *America as Americans See It.* New York: Harcourt, Brace, 1932.

A.M. Sakolski, *The Great American Land Bubble.* New York: Harper & Brothers, 1932.

Paul Sann, *The 20s: The Lawless Decade.* New York: Crown, 1957.

Robert Sklar, ed., *The Plastic Age (1917–1930).* New York: George Braziller, 1970.

Bryan B. Sterling and Frances N. Sterling, *Will Rogers' World.* New York: M. Evans, 1989.

Gordon Thomas and Max Morgan-Witts, *The Day the Bubble Burst: A Social History: The Wall Street Crash of 1929.* Garden City, NY: Doubleday, 1979.

John Tipple, ed., *Crisis of the American Dream: A History of American Social Thought 1920–1940.* New York: Pegasus, 1968.

Wyn Craig Wade, *The Fiery Cross: The Ku Klux Klan in America.* London: Simon and Schuster, 1987.

T.H. Watkins, *The Hungry Years.* New York: Marian Wood, 1999.

Edmund Wilson, *The American Earthquake.* Garden City, NY: Doubleday Anchor, 1958.

———, *The American Jitters: A Year of the Slump.* Freeport, NY: Books for Libraries Press, 1968.

Index